GW00775874

DEAD CLIENTS
DON'T PAY

DEAD CLIENTS
DON'T PAY
THE BODYGUARD'S MANUAL

LEROY THOMPSON

PALADIN PRESS
BOULDER, COLORADO

Dead Clients Don't Pay
The Bodyguard's Manual
by Leroy Thompson
Copyright © 1984 by Leroy Thompson

ISBN 0-87364-287-2
Printed in the United States of America

Published by Paladin Press, a division of
Paladin Enterprises, Inc., P.O. Box 1307,
Boulder, Colorado 80306, USA.
(303) 443-7250

Direct inquiries and/or orders to the above address.

All rights reserved. Except for use in a review, no
portion of this book may be reproduced in any form
without the express written permission of the publisher.

Neither the author nor the publisher assumes
any responsibility for the use or misuse of
information contained in this book.

CONTENTS

1. A Bodyguard's Training 1

2. Professional Assignments 13

3. A Bodyguard's Weapons 23

4. Vehicular Security 57

5. High-Profile, Low-Profile Bodyguard 71

6. Area Security 83

7. Minimizing the Threat 103

1. A Bodyguard's Training

ALTHOUGH THERE ARE SCHOOLS—A few of them quite good—that purport to train bodyguards, no established criteria exist for what constitutes the optimum training for the bodyguard. No licensing agency regulates the profession and sets the standards, though in the United States and some other countries, bodyguards are often licensed through the same bureaus that grant private investigator's licenses. There are, however, certain characteristics and types of training that are most beneficial to the bodyguard.

Physically, the male bodyguard (BG) should be relatively large to allow for the times when physical "presence" can prevent trouble. In a nightspot, for example, a BG can't whip out his trusty fourteen-gun (six-guns are for cowboys; 14-shot Brownings are for BGs) and start blasting away because a drunk is annoying his client. In such situations, firmly grabbing the belligerent individual by the upper arms, lifting him about a foot off the floor, and then gently setting him aside is often more impressive than a real show of force. Such an action is a show of *strength* which hints at *potential force* but which is relatively nonaggressive. Of course, one must be prepared to deal with a truly belligerent individual as well, and in that case, the conflict should be ended as quickly as possible, preferably with one punch, strike, or snap-kick.

I am only five foot, ten inches, but as a former competitive weight lifter and judoka who weighs in at 195 pounds,

1

I am bulky enough to interpose between a client and a threat with authority but not so large that I stand out in a crowd. The disadvantage of a BG with defensive-tackle dimensions is that he is very easy to spot, thus drawing unwanted attention to his employer and making himself a more obvious target should potential attackers wish to neutralize him prior to going after his client. With certain exceptions in which a huge, physically imposing BG is an advantage, the best size for a male BG is probably between five foot eight inches and six foot two inches in height and 180 and 225 pounds in weight. There are, of course, excellent BGs who are larger or smaller than these specifications, but as a rule, average to a few inches above average height is necessary not only for physical presence but also so that the BG can see a potential threat over a crowd.

Quite often, someone will attempt to counter the need for size in a BG by mentioning the martial artist who may not be large. Martial arts ability does not prevent the trouble, however, unless the BG walks around wearing his gi, and this is obviously not practical. Size is a preventive, and though the smaller black belt may be able to rip the larger BG to pieces, his physical size will not keep someone from taking a poke at the client. And for a client under public scrutiny, such an attempt will bring unwanted publicity. The smaller individual will not be able to run interference in crowds as effectively either. Martial arts are an excellent skill for the BG, but a six-foot black belt is far more valuable as a BG than a five-foot black belt.

For the female BG, physical size is not as important since she is frequently hired because she is less obtrusive. Hand-to-hand combat training, however, is a virtual necessity for the female BG to help offset her smaller stature.

In fact, hand-to-hand training is important for both male and female BGs, and I've known competent BGs with specialties in virtually every martial art, including one kendo man who carried a short sword as one of his weapons. Rumor had it that this Japanese fellow had formerly been a BG for a yakuza.

Hwarang Do is one of the most effective martial arts for the BG because of the diverse methods of mayhem it teaches. Jujitsu is also good because techniques normally associated with both judo and karate are taught. One of the most effective BGs in the world received his training in aikido and swears that his effective use of ki is one reason for his success. Escrima or one of the other martial arts that stresses blade use, as Hwarang Do does, can also be very useful. More traditional, western hand-to-hand arts such as savate, fencing, wrestling, or boxing can be beneficial as well. The BG wants to avoid fisticuffs if at all possible since threats should be kept as far from a client as possible. But if it does come down to hand-to-hand combat, any training and experience is very, very useful since the BG wants to end the conflict immediately. Combat sports will also help the BG overcome any squeamishness about physical confrontations. He must be ready to act quickly and decisively to counter a threat, and fear of physical conflict can cause a fatal hesitation.

Along with training in the martial arts, a good BG must remain physically fit. Not only does general physical fitness keep his reactions sharp, it also keeps him more employable. Few people want to trust their lives to someone who looks like a slob. Looks, of course, can be deceiving. One of the minor Greek shipping magnates used to have a BG who looked to be a middleaged butterball but who had actually been one of Greece's foremost wrestlers. He didn't carry an ounce of fat, and anyone who underrated him made a big mistake. This fellow was the only professional I have ever known who carried a Luger pistol, one which he had supposedly acquired from a dead officer while serving with the partisans in World War II.

Training, of course, must include more than just physical skills. A college education is certainly not a necessity for a BG, but for many of the better jobs, a high level of poise, intelligence, and sophistication are necessary, and a university education can help. Many times a man is hired because he can mix at social gatherings and talk intelligently to the guests; thus he remains undercover since BGs are often thought of as "big and dumb." Whatever one's educational background, though, he should make it a point to gain some knowledge of the manners, mores, and interests of the people whom he will guard.

Military or police training is essential for the top-level BG. This is true not only because of the skills one gains during such training but also because of the experience and maturity one normally gains. Generally, top BGs are at least thirty years old, though there are exceptions, of course. A bit of age normally means one will have more experience and thus better judgement. Clients also have more confidence in someone with maturity.

Law enforcement experience most applicable for the BG is usually through agencies which perform the protective function. Former members of the Secret Service command top salaries because of their reputation for professionalism, intelligence, training, and dedication. The only criticism of ex-Secret Service agents I have ever heard is that in some quarters they are viewed as too hesitant to drop an attacker. There is some truth in this view and some misconception. It must be understood that the Secret Service is more concerned about a live protectee than a dead attacker, as all good BGs should be. The Secret Service agent's first concern is shielding the protectee and getting him to safety. As with most U.S. law enforcement training, however, Secret Service training sometimes stresses when *not* to shoot more than when *to* shoot, thus inculcating a certain reluctance to use deadly force. In some countries with high-risk protectees and with a different value of human life, especially the life of a potential assassin, such reluctance is considered a weakness.

Ex-Secret Service agents are probably best suited for assignments in which prevention is paramount, which is in most assignments. They are among the very best in the world at anticipating possibly dangerous situations and avoiding them for their clients. The only disadvantage ex-Secret Service agents have in the preventive sector is their reliance on a large back-up system. Agents are trained to function as part of a large organization having great assets at its disposal. As a result, a lone ex-agent may have to make some adjustment. Being "company men" (not THE "Company"), most ex-Secret Service agents tend to work for security agencies staffed by other ex-government agents, thus maintaining their organizational back-up.

Other established training grounds for BGs include the British Special Branch of Scotland Yard; the French SDECE, DST, or GIGN; the Italian Carabinieri; the Soviet KGB; the United States FBI, DIA, CIA, or NSA (the latter primarily for electronic security positions); the Spanish GEO; the German GSG-9; and many other agencies which are trained in protective, counterintelligence, or counterterrorist methods. Because of the experience gained guarding Charles de Gaulle from the OAS, former French "official" BGs have had a good reputation. It must be remembered, however, that most of the old counter-OAS guards are now in their late forties or older.

Official Italian BGs have sometimes gotten a bad rap because of the number of their protectees—most notably Aldo Moro—lost to terrorist attacks. During the last few years, however, Italian government BGs have improved and are more sought after now for civilian employment. British

Special Branch BGs, unfortunately, do not have an outstanding reputation, especially in their ability to use firearms well under stress. As a result, the best British BGs are often former members of the Special Air Service—the SAS, which will be discussed along with other military units as a training ground for BGs. In all fairness, it should be noted that VIP protection training among the Metropolitan Police and other British police has improved dramatically during the last two years with much assistance coming from the SAS.

Training in normal law enforcement has certain application to work as a BG, but mostly at the low-threat level. The average uniformed police officer is trained—for the most part—to deal with crime after the fact. His concern is prevention through patrolling and punishment through bringing a felon to justice. The BG, on the other hand, works to prevent a threat and to counter a threat if it does materialize. Levels of practical firearms training vary immensely among normal urban police forces, and many ex-police officers are not well enough trained to deal with the types of deadly force situations a BG protecting a high-risk client might encounter.

The primary advantages of a standard police academy/ patrol car/plainclothes background is that one has learned to deal with stress and does have some firearms training. Normally, the ex-police officer will be reasonably well qualified for uniformed estate security work or for protecting low-threat targets. Some police officers, especially those on large, urban police departments in the U.S., have special training in witness protection, mayoral protection, or VIP protection which makes them much more well qualified for work as a BG. Some U.S. marshals are also especially trained for protective work, as are certain members of highway patrol/state police forces assigned to gubernatorial protective units.

Military training can also provide an excellent background for BGs. The British SAS, as already mentioned, provides excellent training. Former members of the counter-terrorist unit who have been through the CQB (close quarters battle) course are especially trained for protective assignments. Many British diplomats on high-risk assignments are, in fact, protected by "former" (one can never be sure) SAS men contracted by the government through one of the security agencies staffed by former SAS men.

Sometimes confused with the SAS is the SBS whose members are very tough and competent, though not, strictly speaking, trained in protective skills. Counterterrorist training in defense of the North Sea oil rigs helps equip former SBS men for certain protective jobs in situations involving yachts, shorelines, or islands (jobs where their special aquatic skills can come in handy). The SBS is a part of the Royal Marine Commandos, many former members of which have joined private security forces to do perimeter or other types of external protective work. One British unit that has produced some estate security professionals is the RAF Regiment, whose members receive a solid background in area security.

Within the U.S. armed forces, there are two units which receive special protective training. The Air Force Security Police have a squadron based near Washington which works with the Secret Service primarily in matters relating to Air Force One or Two. The U.S. Marines also have a limited number of competent men who have been trained to function as plainclothes BGs to U.S. ambassadors. At any one time, only a very small number of Marines on embassy duty have the special qualifications for executive protection. Unfortunately, the excellent Marine firearms training does not normally stress combat handgun usage and is heavily countered by their association with the State Department, which causes them to be very hesitant in using their weapons.

U.S. Air Force Security Policemen, in particular those assigned to SAC headquarters at Offutt AFB, have always had a sound reputation, especially at area security, and are considered good prospects as BGs. Those trained in the Curtis LeMay days were generally known as "bad dudes." Air Force security training, especially under LeMay, ingrained many good habits. During my time in OTS, for example, leaving a personal locker unlocked while out of the room was enough to wash one out. Draconian, to be sure, but one learned the basic tenet that things which are supposed to be secure should be secured. A stint with OSI or being assigned as a BG to a high-ranking officer in a combat zone would even better qualify one as a BG.

Airborne and Ranger qualified Army personnel are good bets on toughness, but their training really has little applicability to protection. The Special Forces, on the other hand, normally incorporates certain training which may be helpful. A demolitions expert, for example, could recognize many types of "infernal machine." Special Forces ambush training gives good grounding in what to look for to spot potential ambush sites. The Air Force Combat Security Police of the Vietnam era—my old unit—were Ranger-trained and were highly skilled in ambush and counterambush, thus giving them some of the same desirable characteristics as ex-members of Special Forces. Members of the Special Forces are also trained to operate individually or in small groups, thus enabling a former "beret" to function as an independent BG. Special Forces weapons training—especially with SMGs and assault rifles—is also very good. Not only can a former weapons leader use the weapons himself, but he is also very skilled at training security force personnel in their usage. A few members of Special Forces have even been assigned to either train or act as BGs for friendly third world officials and have gained actual hands-on BG experience in a high-threat environment. Members of the Delta counterterrorist unit have also received much valuable training. Quite a few ex-members of Special Forces have worked with the CIA or AID and thus gained other experience applicable to protective jobs.

Former CIA "wet" (assassination) operations specialists, Special Forces, SAS, etc. are occasionally employed for *protective reaction* or *first strike* operations. In simple terms, this means a wealthy client hires them to eliminate the threat in advance or to warn someone that if he continues to be a threat, his demise is imminent. At least one agency supplying BGs does so with the understanding that if they lose a client, whoever ordered the hit is "bought and paid for" henceforth. Obviously, this is not a widely broadcast policy, but potential attackers of this agency's protectees normally get the word. At least one fugitive financier is well known for using Cubans formerly employed by the CIA as enforcer/ bodyguards. Reportedly, some of these men are used for first strike ops.

As with the SBS, the U.S. Navy's SEALs find themselves in demand for BG jobs which require the ability to check boat hulls for explosive devices, patrol around an island, etc. SEAL weapons, hand-to-hand, and ambush training are all among the best in the world, and they have a carry-over benefit for the BG. Although SEALs don't receive special training in protective functions, a relatively high proportion of ex-SEALs turn up in the BG game, and they are normally real pros.

Perhaps more because of the nature of the individuals who join the French Foreign Legion than by any specialized training they receive, many ex-Legionnaires end up working as BGs, though rarely in the higher level executive protection positions. One factor that legislates against ex-Legionnaires in such executive protective positions is—rightly or wrongly—the reputation many ex-Legionnaires have for being alcoholic and hence unreliable. On the positive side,

Legionnaires have a mystique that appeals to certain employers and that sometimes makes them effective in high-profile situations, since they also have a reputation for not fearing death. This works in their favor because most attackers hesitate to go against someone who might be a "berserker" or a "kamikaze." At least one ex-Legion officer married a very wealthy "colon" and acts as troubleshooter and BG for his father-in-law. The good life has not made him soft either. Other ex-Legionnaires acted as BGs for the hierarchy of the outlawed OAS and were involved in some bitter clashes with the men of Section 5 of the SDECE.

Ex-members of the Federal Republic of Germany's GSG-9 make excellent BGs because their training emphasizes not just physical but mental skills as well. Members of GSG-9 are trained not only to counter a terrorist threat but also to anticipate one. High-speed driving is a part of GSG-9 training, but using a former member of this unit as a chauffeur would certainly be a waste of talent. GSG-9 marksmanship standards under stress conditions are among the highest in the world, and this has great application for the BG. Ex-members of GSG-9 normally operate very effectively in low-profile assignments since they have been trained to blend into any type of milieu in which they might have to operate. Some, for example, have been well trained as waiters, a useful skill for guarding at a social function. It should be noted that few former members of GSG-9 turn up on the "open market." Instead, they tend to gravitate to positions which are government sanctioned.

There are, of course, other military and police units which can give the potential BG useful training. Whatever the specific background, however, it should have prepared him both physically and mentally for a protective job. Physically, he needs to have received hand-to-hand combat training and be in excellent condition. Airborne, Ranger, and other "elite" training is useful because it will have developed both mental and physical toughness. Skill with weapons is another facet of training that is essential for the BG. A potential BG cannot rest on his laurels where firearms are concerned. He must constantly practice to keep these skills sharp. Training at one of the better practical shooting schools, especially at one that has experience training BGs, can also be very helpful.

Mentally, the BG should be trained in terrorist and criminal modus operandi. If possible, he should also have some training in explosives, investigation, surveillance, area security, psychology, first aid, languages, and electronic security. The smart BG can avoid as much as 90 percent or more of potential threats by knowing what to watch for. Such knowledge is normally gained by experience, hence the very real advantage of military or police protective and security training is experience. Unfortunately, most schools training BGs emphasize countering a threat much more than anticipating it, and the focus is placed on shooting, martial arts, and escape and evasion driving. The perception is often too physical, and this results in an overemphasis on physical training, which is necessary, of course, but not to the exclusion of mental training.

Much information can be gained by working with experienced professionals early in one's career. For this reason, it is often useful to begin by working as part of an area security force. One will normally get a chance to work with the BGs handling the close-in protective assignment and to pick their brains. They won't tell everything they know—no pro will—but they'll usually impart useful information. One briefing from a real pro on how to watch a crowd, for example, can be an eye-opener—literally.

Though there is no set "curriculum" for the BG, there are skills which have universal application to protective assignments. Anyone who wants to be a BG should do everything he can to gain these skills.

2. PROFESSIONAL ASSIGNMENTS

BASICALLY, THE BG'S ASSIGNMENTS will break down into two categories: protection of a client's physical person or protection of an area containing the client. Within these broad categories, assignments can be broken down further into protection against assassination, protection against kidnapping, protection from intruders, and protection of an area. Normally, all of these functions will be required to a greater or lesser degree depending upon the client.

In simple terms, when protecting political figures, one's primary concern will be assassins with political kidnappers as a secondary threat. When protecting high ranking executives, kidnapping will normally be a greater threat than assassination. When protecting entertainers or other "personalities," keeping unwanted visitors (i.e. fans and newsmen) away from them will often be the foremost duty, with protection from kidnappers or assassins taking on secondary importance. Because of the deaths of Sharon Tate and John Lennon among others, many entertainers are extremely paranoid about being murdered. It should be noted, however, that had either Tate or Lennon had a real pro working in their behalf, they would be alive today, and there would be a few dead potential killers. A few years ago members of the "Grand Ole Opry" began hiring BGs because of a rash of suspicious deaths among the country music community in Nashville. An interesting upswing in the hiring of BGs by *Playboy* playmates occurred after the murder of Dorothy Stratten in

August, 1980. Still, the BG protecting an entertainer normally does not have to deal with assassins as often as does the BG protecting a politico. BGs working for members of the "landed gentry" will usually find that kidnapping and murder/robbery are the two primary threats concerning their clients.

Often, the BG will be assigned to guard members of the family of the client since wives and children are prime targets of terrorists. The late Shah of Iran's extensive family have been very good customers for BGs, as have members of the former royal family of Libya. On the more mundane level, many political figures are worried about their children, and more than one BG has spent years shepherding a charge through school. One Middle Eastern BG I know even managed to get his MBA while his charge was in undergraduate school in the U.S. Although protection of children is not my specialty, I have drawn this assignment from time to time because I have worked as a secondary and college instructor. As with the bodyguard/chauffeur, the bodyguard/tutor is better as a back-up than as the primary protector.

Normally, the most prestigious and highest paid position is as personal BG to a VIP. There may be an entire protective force assigned to the individual, but the personal BG is the one who is the client's shadow and who is in charge of the rest of the security force. The personal BG's duties will usually include being near the protectee at all times a threat appears likely and being available at most other times. Unless specialists are retained for electronic or other matters, he will also be in charge of checking rooms, vehicles, etc. for explosives or bugging devices before approving them for the client. If a team is employed, however, it is better to have a technician to handle these matters since any time spent on such duties detracts from the personal BG's primary mission— watching for hostile individuals. The personal BG will normally also have input into travel or other arrangements so

The bodyguard on duty outside a continental townhouse assumes the "bodyguard stance" as a suspicious vehicle approaches. Note that his right hand is inside his coat so that his weapon can be instantly drawn. He carries three guns and a knife on his person, and a submachine gun is positioned just inside the window.

that he can attempt to counter security problems which might occur. The U.S. Secret Service, for example, makes incredibly detailed security arrangements for a presidential visit. A private security force will not have anything like the resources of the Secret Service, but such simple matters as knowing which route into a city from an airport offers the least likelihood of ambush can be extremely important. Once again, a relatively large protective force can boast an advance man who goes ahead to take care of such planning, but otherwise the personal BG will handle these arrangements in his "spare" time.

The personal BG will often become the de facto or official head of security, which means he will be in charge of hiring, firing, training, and inspecting the security force and security devices. As a result, the personal BG must have a working knowledge of everything from guard dogs to infrared sensors so that he can intelligently evaluate the security setup he's working within. Occasionally a BG with extensive experience will be hired as the personal BG of a third world entrepreneur or diplomat. Part of the BG's assignment may then be to train the indigenous security force of the employer.

Sometimes the personal BG will be the entire security force. In this case, he must handle everything himself and must reconcile himself to the fact that he can't be everywhere. This is a situation in which it is best to impress upon a high-risk client the need for at least a backup in the person of a chauffeur trained to act as a secondary BG. If the chauffeur can take care of checking the vehicle for sabotage and also lay down covering fire if ambushed, a good deal of responsibility will be lifted from the BG's shoulders. I still prefer vehicles with alarm systems to inhibit tampering though, and I still like to check a vehicle which has been sitting.

Instead of being the one personal protector, quite often the BG will be hired as one of two, three, or four close-in personal security people. An advantage of this system is that one can get a bit of time off at night or when the protectee is sleeping. In a three-man unit, for example, all three will normally accompany the protectee when in high-visibility, high-risk situations. Assuming that the protectee is at a meeting of some sort, one BG will remain outside, one will cover the hall leading to the meeting room, and the third will either be in the meeting room or outside the doorway. If others attending the meeting have BGs of known ability, then duties can be split with them. This is especially true since one BG is usually enough to watch a group of vehicles.

Assuming a twenty four-hour protective effort is in effect, one BG can be off-duty and away from the protectee's residence at night, one can be off-duty but resting or sleeping at the residence, and the third BG can be on duty. If the client lives on a large estate and there is not an estate security force, however, one man will be spread rather thin.

Normally, when working in conjunction with other pros, duties will be divided according to each BG's particular expertise. For example, I usually work close to the protectee, though if another member of the team has special qualifications such as language, he or she may take the close-in assignment. *Close-in* specifies the BG who moves along with the protectee while the others take stationary positions watching for potential attackers. If one BG is especially knowledgeable about technical matters, he will normally handle explosive and bug sweeps. A female BG as part of the team can often blend into the background as a secretary and accompany the protectee while attracting less attention than her male colleagues. If the protectee is female, then, of course, the female BG can accompany her many places the male BG cannot.

Interestingly enough, some protectees are unwilling to hire multiple personal BGs, not because of the additional expense but because of their unwillingness to trust that many

ILLUSTRATION BY KEN MACSWAN

The bodyguard must learn to protect his employer while he prepares to engage his assailant. A gunfighter's crouch must be avoided, and the weak hand should be used to push the client to protection. Here the guard's body shields his protectee while pointing toward the attacker.

people. Some exiled politicos have a permanent contract out on them from the present regime of their former homelands and, as a result, have little trust in security people who have not gained their confidence. The Americans and the British have fairly good reputations for "staying bought," but even so, many high-risk clients are distrustful. As a result, a good BG may also have to know of three or four highly trustworthy colleagues he can call in to augment his services if needed. As an example of the problem some ex-politicos have with trust, I have one former client who still insists on hiring me to take over when his regular BG has to be away for any reason—despite the fact that I take only selected assignments these days and charge high rates. By the time expenses are paid, this individual is paying three times what he could hire competent local talent for, but he's buying peace of mind.

Less experienced BGs will often be hired as part of a larger protective force and will usually handle perimeter duties. They will be to the protectee what picket destroyers are to the aircraft carrier. Their job is to detect, as early as possible, a potential attacker and neutralize him or, failing that, warn the inner protective ring of security personnel. These less experienced BGs are often the ones who will ride in the backup car, who will throw a cordon around a building or area to seal off admittance, and who will take care of the outside functions at social gatherings. Quite often these men will double as the personal BG assigned to the client's wife, children, or important visitors after they have proven themselves.

In the case of clients who have a large estate or ranch rather than an urban townhouse or apartment, there may also be a security force charged with area security. A bodyguard/butler can often handle the function of securing a smaller urban residence in the absence of the protectee and BGs. Unlike the BG, area security personnel do not normally travel with the protectee but remain at the estate to keep it a secure haven. Area security personnel can range in ability and training from the level of rent-a-cops to the level of elite strike units as well trained as some military commando units. Unfortunately, the former rather than the latter predominates, though if the client is willing to pay to hire at least a few pros for this force, its performance can greatly improve. Often, trained BGs will act as the reaction force for an estate protective unit when the protectee is in residence. If the area security force is primarily made up of locals who have not had military or police background, hiring a reaction force of pros is very important so that a threat can be met as quickly as possible and prevented from reaching the main house. Although it's not usually a stated reason, the BGs are also used as a reaction force to "stiffen" the locals.

If estate security is taken seriously by a high-risk target, then the whole guard force may be composed of highly trained individuals including dog handlers, electronic warning and surveillance system specialists, patrol units, and a reaction force. Normally, security of the main house itself will fall to the personal BGs. Although I usually work as part of the close-in protective staff, I have also worked with area security personnel since I have had quite a bit of training and experience at ambush and counterambush techniques. As a result, I have—in situations where an infiltration attempt was anticipated—led an ambush unit, though afterwards it was reported that a routine security patrol had discovered intruders while on a sweep of the premises. Lying in wait for bad guys with the intent to help them die for their beliefs is normally frowned on by authorities in most places.

Rarely, and then only if the BG has had experience in special or elite military units, there are assignments available in "private armies." Although the employer in these cases isn't usually a warlord in the tradition of 1930 China (though one

The bodyguard may be called upon to handle many duties. The photo at top shows dress for a paramilitary operation, and the bodyguard carries a Gerber, an AR-180, and his Browning Hi-Power. Below, the bodyguard aids the chauffeur in checking the vehicle for tampering.

acquaintance claims to have worked for a Chinese warlord in the Golden Triangle as late as the 1960s), there are a few employers with the wealth, power, and land holdings to hire a security force of twenty-five or more men trained and armed as light infantry. In at least two cases I know about, such forces are based on private islands owned by the protectee. Such island protective forces—because of the aquatic nature of the protective function—tend to draw heavily upon former members of the U.S. Navy SEALs, USMC Recons, British Royal Marine Commandos or SBS, Italian Incursori, etc. As with estate security units, private armies often consist of a core of professionals augmented by a few dozen "indigs."

There are many specialized areas in which the bodyguarding function is provided in addition to other duties. Bodyguard/pilots and bodyguard/chauffeurs, for example, specialize in offering security along with special vehicular skills. Escape and evasion driving are the chauffeur's primary marketable skills, however. Large agencies specializing in executive protection may also have what the U.S. Secret Service terms "protective research specialists" who are trained in identifying potential threats. Usually, however, these psychological specialists are not field BGs. They leave the dirty work to the hard men.

The best BGs are normally ready and qualified to undertake a broad spectrum of assignments. Overspecialization can result in missing something important at a critical time because one is concentrating too heavily on only one aspect of a protective problem. Having worked on many types of protective assignments usually allows one to anticipate more readily the possible threats. Diversity also better prepares the BG for having to handle everything himself for those times when he's the only man on the job.

3. A Bodyguard's Weapons

It HAS BEEN SAID THAT A DEADLY MAN is far more fearsome than a deadly weapon. Deadly weapons alone cannot make someone a professional, but by nature of the threat a BG is hired to counter, deadly weapons are an absolute necessity for him. Though his wits may remain his best weapon, firearms—and on occasion the blade—must be chosen with careful consideration. Once chosen, these weapons must be mastered. Although specific situations call for special weapons with special characteristics, the professional BG will generally find that his most valuable weapon will be the handgun, followed, in order of importance, by the submachine gun, the fighting shotgun, and the assault rifle. Assorted other weapons, including knives, nunchaku, etc., also have their places, but the firearm is preeminent since the BG wants to counter a threat at the greatest possible distance from the protectee.

HANDGUNS

Anyone with a good general knowledge of firearms realizes that the handgun is the least effective of the four types of firearms mentioned, yet here it rates as tops for the BG. Why? The handgun is the most concealable, for one thing, and the BG frequently guards a client in situations where no weapon should be visible. The handgun is also the most portable, allowing the BG to have a hand free to push his client behind cover while drawing to counter a perceived threat. Although most shooters today, including myself, use some type of two-handed firing technique, the handgun is still a one-hand weapon, which is important to the BG, who has two basic jobs—to remove the protectee from the threat and to counter the threat. The handgun is also a selective weapon. If an attack from a crowd must be countered, the handgun offers a far better chance of eliminating the attacker without littering the landscape with innocent bystanders than does the SMG or the riot gun. If, however, the whole crowd is the threat and one's client packs the political clout to handle the ramifications, trot out the choppers and start "rockin' and rollin'."

The handgun may be the best individual weapon for the BG working in urban areas or highly developed countries, but it is also the least forgiving one. The handgun demands constant practice just to retain one's competency. At a minimum, 100 rounds per month must be fired through one's primary handgun, and when one is in a situation where range facilities are available, at least 100 rounds per week should be expended.

When sophisticated range facilities are available, practice should include shots at moving targets, at targets in vehicles, and at targets behind cover. Practice should also include firing from vehicles, firing on the move, firing from behind cover, and making rapid magazine changes. Situations should be set up involving multiple targets and "hostage" targets, in which only a small portion—usually the head—of the bad guy is presented. Speaking of head shots, many criminals and terrorists are now aware of the advantages of body armor, and as a result I practice the technique of firing the first shot at the center of mass (i.e. the chest cavity) and the second shot at the head. This double-hit system should be practiced until it becomes automatic. Even against a subject wearing body armor, the impact of the first hit from a

Handgun expertise should allow the bodyguard to hit the mark in rapid firing at twenty-five yards. At top, the guard practices head shots. Training with a military or police organization or at a private shooting school is beneficial. The situation in the lower photo simulates encounters where shooting through auto windows and doors is essential.

powerful handgun should create enough trauma to allow the split second needed for the coup de grace.

Pop-up targets, including friend and foe targets, should also be used if possible. The BG must be able to make split-second, shoot-don't-shoot decisions, and having to identify a target as a possible assailant or not helps train one to make this decision. I can think of two cases when I was guarding high-risk clients and a threatening gesture, seen from the corner of my eye, caused me to draw my gun and level it on target with the safety off, without my even consciously thinking about the act. In each case, the decision not to fire was made instantly and correctly. Before consciously considering the situation, I had evaluated the acts as nonhostile and had exercised restraint. Had a weapon been shown, the potential attacker would have been fired at just as reflexively.

It is normally a precept in training one to shoot "tactically" that the closest target should be engaged first. As a general rule, this is true, but the BG must train himself to evaluate threats and react accordingly. An assailant at five yards with a .32 auto or knife is less of a threat than one at twenty yards with an RPG7 (though admittedly the RPG is a notoriously inaccurate weapon despite propaganda to the contrary) or a fully automatic weapon. Having pop-up or surprise targets at varying distances with different weapons showing is also useful in training one to make split-second decisions. By the way, the SAS technique of telling the protectee to hit the ground by using his or her first name should be practiced in such situations. Normally, a person will respond more quickly to his first name when under stress than his last name. Hence, no matter how polite the BG normally is to his employer, practice telling him to take cover using his first name.

Shooting in IPSC competition whenever one's assignments permit is highly recommended. Although there are certain artificial elements to IPSC competition—such as changing magazines when one's gun is not dry, shooting under pressure, bringing one's gun into action from the leather, and shooting weak-handed—all offer good training. It should be stressed, however, that one is not shooting to win the match but for training, and "gamesmanship" should be avoided, as should trick leather or other gimmicks which one could not use in the real world. Shoot the same gun from the same leather that will be used when on assignment.

Choice of holster is also an important consideration for the BG. Although there are times when one is working high profile that concealment is not important, the BG will usually be working in a business suit, and concealability will be very important. The gun must also be positioned for fast access and preferably for access with either hand. At least once, I have had to fight off a physical assault with my right hand while drawing with my left, thus proving empirically the value of a dual access holster. The most suitable holster for the BG dressed in a business suit is a crossdraw located over the hipbone. A rig which fits relatively close to the body, worn under a suit cut to fit over it, offers good concealability, yet very fast access. Standing with one's hand under his coat, resting on his gun, can save even more time using the crossdraw. This type of holster is also perfect for the "bodyguard's stance," in which one stands with his back against a secure wall, with his arms crossed and his hand resting on his handgun. In a high-threat situation, the gun can even be drawn and kept under the coat.

My second choice is a down-slanting shoulder holster which offers many of the same advantages as the crossdraw but is not as accessible to the weak hand. A well-designed shoulder holster is, however, the best way to conceal a very bulky handgun (normally a poor choice for a BG anyway). A well-designed shoulder rig may also be the most comfortable

The crossdraw is especially useful since it is accessible to either hand and allows the fastest draw from under a coat. This compact holster from Horseshoe Leather positions the Detonics for maximum concealment yet allows it to be quickly drawn into action.

method for carrying a handgun. The crossdraw holsters made by Horseshoe Leather slant the handgun properly so that it does not dig into the ribs as one sits, yet the gun is accessible both standing or sitting. Horseshoe Leather also custom built a double shoulder holster system for me so that I can carry a Browning Hi-Power under the left arm and an H&K P7 under the right arm. The P7 was chosen as the left hand gun because its squeeze-cocker system allows it to be used ambidextrously. Both of the holsters slant the gun butt downward at the angle I prefer for easy access. I also use a Jackass shoulder system which is designed to work almost like a vest. A double magazine pouch rides under the strong side arm. This is a real boon when working in situations where one must remain alert even when off duty. I hang the Jackass with the Hi-Power and two spare magazines on the bed. Then I can hurriedly go into action, since just by grabbing the Jackass, I have my gun and forty rounds of ammo.

If a hip holster is chosen, a backrake is usually faster than a frontrake when worn under a coat. Ankle holsters are usually only good for carrying one's number-three gun since they tend to be slow. Women BGs normally favor a shoulder holster or vest with built-in holster designed for their physical differences, though I know one woman who uses a thigh holster worn on the inside of her left thigh and who has developed a very fast right hand draw from this rig. Obviously, she wears dresses or skirts rather than trousers. It must also be admitted that this female—who at last report was pulling down $50,000 plus per annum guarding a top European executive—had such sensational legs that watching her demonstrate her draw was a real treat—that is, if one wasn't the target because she could shoot very well indeed. The purse is normally not a good place for the female BG to carry her weapon since she can be separated from it too easily.

I have frequently taken jobs where it was not feasible to travel with my personal handguns and as a result have worked with locally procured ordnance. This, of course, has the disadvantage of limiting one's familiarity with the weapon. In such situations, one should insist on a range session to check the gun's functioning and accuracy. Don't be afraid to demand a different weapon, too, if the one issued is unsatisfactory. I once fired every gun in a security agency's arsenal and turned them all down. Finally I ended up with the personal handgun of the firm's director. Just getting the agency to arrange a test-fire session was like pulling teeth, but it was necessary, and one has to have the confidence to insist when personal weapons are concerned.

One method used by many professionals who work all over the world is to keep six or so handguns strategically located about the globe either in safe deposit boxes or stored with friends. Once again, the political clout of one's client helps determine the ease of transporting ordnance. It is a point that should be discussed up front. A globe-trotting BG should learn as much as he can about international firearms laws. Working through an agency licensed in the country one will be operating in often cuts through red tape. Working through the country's government sometimes cuts even more, though not always. Another method used by some third world countries, if one is guarding a "politico" or "entrepreneur" with clout, is to issue a diplomatic passport under an assumed name so that "packing" isn't a problem when crossing international borders. If it's necessary to drop someone, diplomatic immunity may come in handy, especially when the persona identified on the passport doesn't really exist and can vanish into obscurity.

In some countries, a handgun purchase permit is hard to get, but when granted, it is also considered a carry permit. In such cases, it is useful to apply for a permit and buy a gun locally if one's employer can help cut the red tape.

In the U.S., one must try to sort out the myriad handgun ordnances. Once again, working through a local agency can be helpful, though private operatives (read that rent-a-cops) must be locally licensed. Another ploy occasionally used, but rarely admitted to, is for the client to arrange to have his BG made a deputy sheriff. Many people who need BGs are large political contributors and may be able to call in such favors from the party apparatus. I had one friend who used to arrange to be appointed "Special Deputy in Charge of Handgun Instruction." He usually ran a day or two session in practical shooting techniques for the local constabulary and almost invariably did such a good job that he was offered a regular position on the force.

Some states will also honor one's home state "carry" permit, but that's usually a touchy subject. Once again the details of legally carrying a firearm should be worked out with an employer in advance.

Airport security procedures are the bane of the BG's existence, and most high-risk targets have learned to fly on private planes so that their watchdogs can go armed. If commercial airlines are flown, the weapons must go in the luggage unless a diplomatic passport and a convenient diplomatic pouch have been arranged. Some professionals have learned that a S&W Model 38 with the ammo elsewhere will occasionally make it through metal detectors, but it's not worth the potential hassles involved. A former employer who owns a piece of his country's national airline uses the interesting and practical expedient of having his BG appointed the official security agent on whatever flight he's traveling on. Since he hires only top pros and pays them himself, the airline gets excellent anti-hijack protection for free.

The handgun chosen by the BG should have certain important characteristics. Most of all, it must be highly reliable.

Malfunctions cannot be tolerated. The weapon must also be highly accurate to at least twenty-five yards. In addition, the handgun must have adequate stopping power to put an opponent down with one solid hit. Since a BG may have to face multiple assailants, the weapon must also allow for fast recovery so that multiple targets can be neutralized swiftly. Firepower (i.e. large cartridge capacity) and quick reload capability will also help counter the threat of multiple attackers. The BG's handgun must also be a good compromise between concealability and size. A reasonably sized gun is necessary so that performance is not lost. Generally, an automatic pistol of 9mm, .38 Super, or .45 ACP is the best choice for the BG, though in certain limited situations, a magnum revolver may have advantages.

AUTOMATICS

Browning Hi-Power: The Hi-Power is not only my top choice; it is also the most widely used handgun in the world by professionals who shoot for keeps. It is no accident that the SS in World War II, MACV/SOG in Vietnam, and the SAS in counter-terrorist ops and in the Falklands have all chosen the big Browning. The Hi-Power offers extreme reliability and durability. It is also so widely distributed that one can get parts about anywhere should they be needed. Accuracy is adequate if not pinpoint with the Browning, though factory sights—both fixed and adjustable—leave something to be desired. The factory adjustable sights should be avoided at all costs since their high profile makes them very likely to snag on a coat lining while drawing under pressure. S&W K-frame revolver sights installed on a Hi-Power prove to be a better choice. Other gunsmithing suggested for the Hi-Power includes a compact ambidextrous safety—I use the M-S Safari one—and beveling of the magazine well. Incorporating the

Nite-Site system makes it possible to align the sights even in complete darkness.

Another real advantage of the Hi-Power is its 14-round capacity. With two spare magazines, this gives forty rounds of ready-access ammo should it be necessary to lay down heavy fire if ambushed. I normally carry at least one spare magazine charged with metal-case, high-velocity ammo in case it is necessary to engage an assailant who is firing from inside a vehicle. Special "armor piercing" 9mm's are even better for this contingency.

The 9mm round leaves something to be desired as a manstopper, but modern, jacketed, hollow-point ammo goes a long way towards improving the 9mms stopping power. I keep my Hi-Power loaded with hollow points unless local law forbids them or unless a situation arises in which full metal case ammo is preferable. A second 9mm can be carried as a back-up and kept loaded with penetrating ammo. The great advantage of the 9mm is its ready availability all over the world, though there are a few countries where its use by civilians is prohibited. Frequently, however, especially if one is working for a "politico," these prohibitions will be waived.

A final advantage of the Hi-Power is psychological rather than physical. The big Browning is recognized worldwide as a pro's gun which gives its wielder a certain amount of status with both his employer and with any opponent scouting the situation for a possible attack. The sight of the Hi-Power coming into play is a slight deterrent, though it should be understood that the BG does not carry his weapon as a threat but as an actuality. Still, in a couple of tight situations involving thugs or other ne'er-do-wells in far-off places with strange sounding names, I have prevented trouble by giving a quick glimpse of the Hi-Power. Potential muggers have been known to melt back into alleys at its sight or upon realizing that, if necessary, it would be used. Professional assassins,

My principle handgun is the Browning Hi-Power. The one at top has an S&W K-frame rear sight, an ambidextrous safety, and a well-beveled magazine. The holster from Horseshoe Leather is my preferred choice. Shown below are two Detonics autos that are useful because of their compactness. At top is a MK VI .38 Super; below is an MC-1 .45 ACP.

The superconcealable gun shown at top is a Seecamp LWS-25 auto, perfect for a pocket gun. Below is a compact Beretta M93R. Used in semiauto mode, the 93R is a large-magazine 9mm pistol; while in three-shot burst mode, it will lay down suppressive fire with one-handed shooting.

however, don't scare just because one carries a good "piece."
Such knowledge might, however, force them to try for one's
client from a little further away, and any distance gained for
maneuver can be important. Yet, as automatic pistols go, the
Hi-Power is relatively concealable because it is flat, despite
its double-row box magazine.

Heckler & Koch P7: The P7 is another 9mm which has two
real advantages for the BG. First, it is very compact, measuring only six-and-one-half inches in overall length, yet has a
capacity of nine rounds and a four inch barrel. This compactness is a direct result of the P7's revolutionary squeeze cocker
system. The squeeze cocker is the other real advantage of
the P7, since it is the only safety necessary on this weapon.
Since the weapon is cocked by squeezing in on the front of
the grip and since it uses a bottom magazine release, the P7
is, in effect, a fully ambidextrous weapon. I normally carry
my P7 as a primary weapon when concealability is an important consideration or as a back-up weapon to my Browning
Hi-Power at other times. The P7's three-dot sighting system
is a very fast acquisition one which allows the weapon to be
aligned quickly and surely. These sights combined with the
squeeze cocker make the P7, with practice, one of the fastest
of all handguns to bring into action. Note closely the words
"with practice," though.

Some professionals who fire thousands of rounds yearly
through their P7s say that they carry a spare trigger return
spring since this is one part which has been known to break
under heavy usage. Virtually all handguns have some part
known to be more fragile than others. Most professionals
learn which key springs, pins, etc. on their weapons receive
the most wear and make up spare parts kits for their
armament.

The P7 is at its best used by the urban BG, since it is a

relatively sophisticated weapon which might have problems if used by the BG working in a private army in the bush. In the P7's favor, I should note that I have carried mine in desert and jungle without any problems.

Detonics MC-1, MK VI: I think very highly of the compact Detonics automatics because they offer so much power in such a small package. These small autos are also designed for extreme reliability and incorporate features such as a throated barrel, polished feed ramp, relieved ejection port, and beveled magazine well, which are normally only available on custom-built combat autos. In the early days of the company's existence, Detonics had a poor reputation for reliability, but I have found that if one follows the break-in procedures suggested for the Detonics pistols, the guns are highly reliable. Extractor problems in the Detonics are easily corrected by replacing the extractor, which is interchangeable with those used in the Colt Government Model or Commander.

The Detonics is available in .45 ACP, 9mm, .38 Super, and .451 Detonics Magnum. The latter is an extremely powerful round but is slow for repeat shots and is not commercially available. Still, when very high knock-down or penetrating power is needed in a small package, it's hard to beat. I use two Detonics autos—an MC-1 .45 and a MK VI .38 Super. The .38 Super offers higher velocity and heavier bullets than the 9mm and is sometimes called the .357 Magnum of auto pistols, though its ballistics aren't really up to those of the .357. The Detonics .38 Super is sometimes carried when high penetration may be needed along with compactness. The .38 Super Detonics is also used in certain South and Central American countries where "military" cartridges such as the 9mm or .45 ACP are forbidden for civilian use. The MC-1 is chosen when the knock-down power of the .45 ACP is desirable and when concealability is necessary. The greatest advantage of the Detonics is its small size, which makes it a good choice for the BG working in low-profile situations.

Both the MC-1 and MK VI are available in stainless steel. Stainless guns have the advantage of being more corrosion resistant, but their reflectivity can be a disadvantage both for concealment under a coat and because one's position can be given away by a shiny gun. Fortunately, though, the very flat grey finish of the MC-1 helps nullify reflectivity.

Seecamp 9mm: This weapon should have been introduced by the time this book goes to press. The Seecamp 9mm offers double-action, first-shot capability and 9mm chambering, yet it is about the size of a Walther PPK. That much power in a small package will make the Seecamp the low-profile BG's dream gun.

CZ75: This Czech product, though hard to come by in the U.S., may well rank right behind the Browning Hi-Power and the Colt Government Model or Commander in popularity with professionals. The CZ75 is reliable and has double-action, first-shot capability, offering a fast initial round and ambidextrous capability. Another real advantage of the CZ is its 16-round capacity which gives it a lot of firepower. Accuracy of the CZ is quite acceptable. Because of the difficulty in getting parts outside of Europe, however, the CZ might not be a good choice for someone working exclusively in the U.S. or certain other parts of the world. Its reputation for durability is fairly good, though.

Colt Government Model or Commander: Next to the Browning Hi-Power, the Colt 1911-type auto is probably the most popular combat auto in the world. Normally chosen in .45 ACP, the Colt offers dependability and reasonable accuracy. Though it is also chambered for the .38 Super and 9mm,

I have found the Colt less reliable in these chamberings than in .45 ACP. Normally, in fact, automatic pistols are most reliable in the caliber for which they were originally designed, and this seems to hold true with the Colt. Parts are widely distributed for the Colt as are gunsmiths who do special work on it. It is easy to get the gun custom-tuned. One has to be careful in having work done on any combat auto, however, to be sure the weapon is not tightened for accuracy at the expense of reliability.

It is my opinion that the Government Model or Commander is not as desirable for the BG as the Hi-Power, the P7, the CZ75, or the Detonics. However, for those skilled in its use, the Colt is an effective weapon which can get the job done. The arguments normally advanced in favor of the Colt are based on its performance in IPSC competition, which, it should be remembered, was designed at least partially to prove the .45's superiority rather than to be an impartial test.

Beretta 92: At first the Beretta 92 seems to be an ungainly weapon, but it has good handling characteristics and is surprisingly accurate. This, combined with its reliability and large magazine capacity, makes it a weapon worthy of consideration. Most, however, will find the Beretta a more difficult weapon to conceal than the Hi-Power or the CZ75, each of which also offers large magazine capacity.

Other large autos worthy of mention include the Astra A80, S&W 439 & 459 (and other versions of these weapons in stainless steel), Sig-Sauer P220 and P225, S.I.G. 210, Walther P-38 and P-5, H&K P9S, and Makarev. All of these powerful automatics (the Makarev less so than the others) offer certain characteristics which might appeal to the BG. Any one of these weapons can be a good choice. Other large autos are the MAB P-15, the Beretta 951 (also the Egyptian version), and the Steyr P-18. One obsolete weapon many professional adventurers keep in their arsenal despite its many faults is the Astra 400. This ungainly weapon is sometimes known as the "garbage eater" because it will function with virtually any 9mm/.38 auto caliber ammo in the world. For the globe-trotting pistol packer this lack of finickiness makes the 400 a useful weapon.

REVOLVERS

Generally, revolvers are a poor choice for the BG. A compact .38 Special revolver such as the S&W Model 36, for example, is really not much more concealable than the H&K P7 which holds four more rounds and has a barrel twice as long. I would choose a revolver only in a situation where extreme knock-down power might be called for or when it might be necessary to fire through a pocket. In the former situations, a four-inch S&W Model 29 or 629 .44 Magnum is probably the best choice. I also use a S&W Model 25-5 .45 Colt revolver which has had the barrel shortened to two-and-one-half inches and has been round-butted to S&W K-frame dimensions. The Colt, S&W, and Ruger .357 Magnum revolvers—especially the Python, Model 19 or 66, and Security Six—are high-quality arms, but their cylinder bulges and small ammunition capacity are severe disadvantages from the BG's standpoint. If a revolver is chosen for occasional or regular use, one must learn to shoot it quickly in the double-action mode and must also learn to make quick reloads using speed loaders.

BACK-UP HANDGUNS

Because not only his life but the lives of others depend on him, the BG normally needs a second hangun. The back-up gun allows for the malfunctioning of the primary weapon

The S&W Model 38 Bodyguard revolver can be fired through a pocket. Note the heavy, semiwadcutter bullet useful in snub-nosed guns at medium velocity. Below is the Walther PPK, a useful back-up weapon. This .32 ACP has its meager stopping power enhanced by the Winchester "Silvertip" cartridges.

or for bringing a second gun into action if the primary gun runs dry. Tactically, a second gun carried in position for a weak-handed draw also grants the BG an element of surprise if the assailant is watching for a draw of the primary arm, though normally an attack will come from cover and which hand the assailant is watching will be a moot point. A variation of this ploy is to have a loaded gun in a coat pocket ready to fire through the pocket if necessary. I use a hammer shrouded S&W 38 "Bodyguard" which is my favorite coat-pocket weapon. On one occasion, I stood behind a client in a receiving line covering each person who approached with the pocketed Model 38. I have also found—as did the U.S. sky marshals—that a cummerbund makes a good place to conceal a flat, compact automatic pistol.

For may years I carried a Walther PPK as my main backup gun, while a Browning .25 auto was a last-ditch third weapon. Occasionally, the PPK or even the tiny Browning became the principal weapon when I was forced to wear swimwear or other athletic clothing to blend in. More than once, the Walther or Browning was taped to my thigh or in the small of my back under light clothing. The Browning was also carried tucked into a jockstrap under tight swimming trunks after checking the safety dozens of times. On that same assignment, which included guarding some children against kidnapping, my female partner attempted to secrete a Benelli .25 auto in the bodice of her swimming suit, but it proved to be a lost cause despite her ample "camouflage."

I always used a rather unique system for carrying the tiny Browning. I wore either Scottish *sgian-dubh* garters or USAF shirt garters and tucked the small auto into a stocking top. Normally, the Scottish garters worked best, but in either case, heavy knit stockings had to be worn. So that I was not lopsided, a sgian-dubh or some other small dagger was usually tucked into the opposite stocking top.

I currently carry a compact, full-power auto as my second gun, frequently the H&K P7 or one of the Detonics. Although the Browning .25 still is used occasionally, the LWS-25 auto has become my favorite because of its double action capability, which I trust far more than the safeties on the typical .25 auto. The Walther TPH, though not readily available in the U.S., is another useful, last-ditch weapon in either .22 l.r. or .25 ACP caliber. The new Seecamp 9mm will probably go a long way towards replacing the PPK for ultra concealment. But I have two .380 PPKs and one .32 PPK stored at critical points around the world, and should the need arise, I will have no qualms about relying on them.

One other .380 which should be mentioned is the Remington Model 51 which has not, unfortunately, been available for almost fifty years. Because of its thin frame and slide, this weapon is very flat, making it highly concealable. It is also one of the best pocket autos ever made. One fancier of the Model 51 as a back-up was Gen. George S. Patton who normally carried one beneath his tunic.

Once the handgun or handguns best suited to one's needs are chosen, however, the bottom line remains mastery of the weapon. Unless one is already highly proficient, thousands of rounds will be expended in this process, and the handgun should become an extension of one's arm.

SUBMACHINE GUNS

The submachine gun has two primary advantages as a BG's weapon. First and foremost, it throws out a lot of lead in a short time, making it an excellent weapon to lay down covering fire while a protectee heads for cover. The SMG is also a good threat weapon, projecting an aura of deadliness which might help discourage "soft-core" attackers. The SMG is especially useful in enclosed areas where its lack of range is not a serious disadvantage. Next to the handgun, the SMG is the most compact firearm in the BG's arsenal. Most pros keep a subgun somewhere in their client's limo for ready use in case of an ambush. Preferring to ride "shotgun" when on duty in a client's vehicle, I have at times used an H&K MP5 mounted on brackets under the dash as a counterambush weapon.

The biggest disadvantage to the SMG is probably a psychological one. Too many BGs—especially those in the employ of African, Asian, or Middle Eastern clients—perceive the SMG as a magic wand which when pointed at the bad guys will make them evaporate. Unfortunately, that's not the case. A thirty-round magazine can be emptied without hitting the target if one doesn't know what he's doing.

I vividly remember visiting the office of an important businessman based in Beirut during the days when it was still the commercial center of the Middle East. Six BGs from the businessman's home country were on duty in an anteroom. The BGs, obviously desert dwellers, seemed a bit disoriented in the city and clutched their Beretta M-12s as if they were talismans. The men, who were no doubt highly competent with the Enfield bolt action rifles they had used since their youth, had obviously not been well trained in the use of their SMGs. They were meant as a threat. Unfortunately, the threat was not enough. This same businessman was killed a few years later despite the size of his protective force. Another target of the same hit squad survived an attempt on his life even though he was protected by a lone, middle-aged, ex-SAS man armed with a Browning and a Sterling. The moral of the story? Don't try to substitute a SMG for a pro.

Assuming the BG has been well trained in the use of the SMG (Special Forces, SAS, GSG-9, et al offer some of the best training, by the way), there are certain considerations which

dictate the choice of weapon. Once again, as with the handgun, there is a trade-off between portability and efficiency.
Normally, the best compromise will be a weapon having a
barrel length of eight to eleven inches and a folding or
telescoping stock. Weapons with a relatively low cyclic rate
(500-600RPM) are the most controllable, thus allowing the
best accuracy. Selective-fire weapons offering single-shot,
burst, or full-auto modes are also preferable for accurate use.

My favorite SMG is the Heckler and Koch MP-5A3. This
version is the telescoping stock version of the standard MP5.
The fact that the MP5 fires from a closed bolt is an aid to
its accurate use. It is also available in specialized versions
which may prove useful to the BG assigned to a high-threat
target. The MP5K, for example, is a super-compact version
which can easily be concealed under a topcoat. One of the
better female BGs (who is assigned to the wife of a high-
ranking foreign government minister) has a large purse
specifically designed to carry an MP5K. Another useful
version is the MP5SD2, which is silenced. Although it is
normally designed for military or counterterrorist use, the
silenced SMG might prove invaluable to the BG in certain
scenarios. Assume, for example, that one could extract himself
and his client from an impending ambush by silently
eliminating one lookout. A silenced weapon would certainly
be useful. Of course, such situations are rarely encountered,
and the additional bulk of a suppressed weapon may hardly
be worth the trouble.

A second choice for a SMG is another German product—
the Walther MPK or MPL. The MPK is especially compact,
just under fifteen inches with the stock folded. That's only
about five inches longer than the S&W Model 29 revolver with
four-inch barrel. The MPK and MPL also have good cyclic
rates of 500 RPM. Other SMGs I have used and been satisfied
with are the Czech VZ-25 (better than the VZ-26 because of

the 9×19mm chambering) and the Beretta M-12. Although I don't use it because of its high cyclic rate, the Ingram M10 is popular with BGs—especially in Latin America—because of its extreme compactness. The Uzi also has a following, but its weight makes it a bit unwieldy.

The MAT-49 still turns up, especially among ex-Legionnaires, while the "Swedish K" also has its own proponents, especially among ex-members of the U.S. Special Forces. A few pros like Sterlings, too. Though some consider the CAR-15 a SMG, I will discuss it as a compact assault rifle.

The SMG is an excellent weapon for the BG, but it should not be chosen with the idea that it will require less practice. If the SMG is carried as the heaviest weapon in a BG's or protective team's arsenal, then enough practice should be undertaken so that combat accuracy can be achieved out to fifty, seventy-five, or even one hundred yards to allow at least a minimal stand-off capability. A selective-fire weapon can be most useful at the longer ranges.

Although I'm not an advocate of one man doing double duty as chauffeur/bodyguard, I do suggest that the chauffeur receive weapons training and be licensed to go armed. He can then act as a back-up if only one BG is protecting the client. For such situations, the SMG is an excellent weapon, allowing the chauffeur to lay down suppressive fire to keep a group of attackers' heads down while getting the vehicle out of the area. Generally, a chauffeur should not leave the vehicle unless it is totally disabled. Thus, the handgun or the SMG is the best choice for use in the confines of a driving compartment.

The SMG is also an excellent primary arm for members of an estate security force concerned with defending a static position. A hallway, for example, can be swept very effectively by a SMG. Dog handlers can also be armed with a SMG since it can be used, if necessary, with one hand while the other hand is controlling the dog's lead.

THE FIGHTING SHOTGUN

Although it has its limitations, the fighting shotgun can be effectively employed by the BG. I prefer the shotgun to the SMG or assault rifle when the shotgun's bulk and lack of range are not considerations. The general all-purpose shotgun for the BG is normally one of the slide-action riot guns with a folding stock or just a pistol grip. Except at very close range, these weapons are really not that effective. Yet they are easy to carry and store in a vehicle. For concealment and work at close range, I do occasionally use a Kimel KPR-12 with pistol grip and find it satisfactory.

For really close work, the old, 20 gauge, double-ten-inch-barreled Auto-Burglar gun is formidable within its limitations. Other short-barreled "whipits" also have their places. One of the world's real pros in the BG game has a double-barreled Holland and Holland 12 gauge with barrels cut to less than a foot and with a pistol grip. This "whipit" is often carried slung beneath a coat, with its owner's hand on the grip through his pocket. Its owner has never lost a client and as long as I have known him, his only armament has been the H&H and a World War II P-38.

One shorty which is quite good is the High Standard M-10. This semiauto weapon was designed from the ground up as a fighter. Its magazine capacity—five rounds—could be larger, but otherwise it's a good weapon. Another real advantage of the M-10 for the BG is that it can be used effectively with one hand.

I like the idea of a semiauto shotgun for combat use and favor the Benelli Police/Military despite its relatively large size. If possible, I keep a Benelli slung beneath the front seat when working from a limo or other vehicle. One of the

Compact assault rifles such as this H&K at top are better for the bodyguard than the SMG since they offer greater range and killing power, yet are compact. Top choice for the guard using an SMG is the H&K MP5. The MP5A3 or MP5K is even better since these 9mms are even more compact.

A favorite fighting shotgun is the Benelli Police/Military 12 gauge semiauto shown here.

carriers designed for use in police vehicles is normally used, and an assault rifle is carried along with the Benelli. A few of the agencies which furnish armored limos have them built so that long gun storage is incorporated, in fact.

Depending on the type of threat anticipated, the shotgun is normally loaded with #1 buck, which offers a good compromise between penetration and pattern. Also useful are "Malaya loads," which were developed by the SAS for counterterrorist use and consist of 00 or 000 buckshot surrounded by BB or #2 shot. These loads are usually used when patrolling an estate or other installation, since they are at their best at close quarters. If an assault rifle is available in the limo, carrying slugs isn't essential, but if the shotgun is the sole long gun, then some slugs are usually carried.

Pump guns are also very useful weapons for the BG. Many people consider them superior to the semiauto since they are less dependent on perfect ammo. A slide action with a double bar is usually the best choice since it offers surer feed and more forceful clearing of empty or jammed cases. Though there are many good pumps around, my favorites are the Ithaca Model 37 (standby of the Special Forces and SEALs in Vietnam) and the Remington 870.

It should be noted, by the way, that if the BG must train a local estate security force in a third world country as part of his duties, the slide action shotgun is a good choice for their primary armament, while a .38 Special revolver can serve as their secondary arm. I have often used the shotgun as the basic arm for a fifteen to twenty-five man security force when training time and armament expense money were at a minimum. In a typical situation, a force of seventeen men might be employed. Five would be on duty in the daytime, five in the evening, and seven at night. The best man on each shift would be armed with a SMG or assault rifle, while the others would carry shotguns. Assuming, of course, the money is there to hire ex-military personnel or more sophisticated locals, a better weapons mix may be achieved.

THE ASSAULT RIFLE

The assault rifle is last on the list of basic small arms for the BG not because it is an ineffective weapon but because its long-range striking power and bulk normally do not make it optimum for personal security work. There are, of course, obvious exceptions. A marksman armed with a scoped assault rifle or sniper's rifle and secreted in a critical location—usually high above the area—can be an excellent counterassassin force. The rifle-armed BG can also function most effectively in the countersniper role. When guarding estates, ranches, islands, mountains, or other private retreats where it might be possible to engage attackers at a distance, the rifle really comes into its own. The selective-fire assault rifle is also an effective weapon against attackers in a vehicle since fully jacketed military ammo offering good penetration is readily available.

I normally don't favor collapsible or folding stocks for shotguns, but I have used them with assault rifles as a substitution for the SMG. A compact, selective-fire assault rifle offers most of the advantages of the SMG but with the increased ballistic efficiency of a rifle cartridge. I have often used an AR-18 (or its semiauto version, the AR-180) for these reasons. Measuring only twenty-eight inches with the stock folded, the AR-18 is a very effective .223 caliber weapon. The CAR-15 is probably more popular than the AR-18, but it is longer with its stock retracted, yet has a shorter barrel.

One other very effective retractable stock assault rifle is the Ruger Mini-14. With some of the folding stocks available for it, the little Ruger collapses to under two feet in overall length. The Mini-14 is also available in stainless steel for use when working aboard ship or in climates where rust can be a problem. The performance of the larger .308 caliber folding stock assault rifles leaves something to be desired. If compactness is a primary consideration, then one of the .223 caliber weapons—CAR-15, AR-18, or Mini-14—is normally chosen. If a .308 is desired, then I opt for either the H&K 91 or the FN-FAL.

Because I have had occasion to act as "second gun" to clients on big game hunting trips, a large-caliber big game rifle has normally been part of my battery. For many years, a Holland & Holland .500/.450 Nitro-Express double rifle that I purchased while I was a student in London served this purpose, but a .375 H&H Whitworth Express rifle now fills this niche. According to a South African I worked with, the .375 with "solids" is just as deadly on automobiles as on Cape Buffalo, a point worth considering for the BG. I have also occasionally carried the .375, some other sporting rifle, or a double barreled Holland & Holland 12 bore shotgun in situations where sporting arms were the only ones which would not call undue attention. On more than one estate in Scotland, for example, some of those "ghillies" walking around with 12 bores over their arms could probably find their way over the Brecon Beacons from memory and might have a well-worn, sand-colored beret tucked away somewhere. Their job title might be gamekeeper, but any unauthorized visitors could conceivably become the "game." One parting comment on sporting rifles is that though I keep a rifle for such uses, in the majority of cases, it has been thousands of miles away when jobs involving hunting trips have come along and I used one of the employer's guns. Hence, by no means should an "elephant gun" be considered a necessary part of the BG's armament.

A final note on firearms and the BG: The professional should take any opportunity to fire assorted weapons from all over the world. It's always good to know weapons other than those normally used in case the situation arises in which one has to work with weapons other than his own. I have, for example, been issued the MAB, Walther P-38, Star, Astra, SIG, Webley, and assorted other weapons. Various rifles, SMGs, and shotguns have also been the only ones available for certain jobs.

Familiarity with weapons is additionally important so that one can recognize the weaponry carried by the opposition and realize its capabilities. This experience can be invaluable in taking evasive or retaliatory action. In one supposedly true story, a BG disarmed an attacker carrying one of the S&W double-action automatics by grabbing his gun hand and pushing the magazine release, thus dumping the magazine and rendering the gun inoperable because of the magazine safety. Fortunately for the BG, he wasn't going up against a real pro, who would probably have disconnected the magazine safety. Still, if the story is true, it illustrates that the BG's experience with weapons gave him a bit of an edge in the scuffle. The question asked, of course, is why did the BG ever let the attacker get that close? In some instances, recognition of weaponry can also aid in identifying the origin of the attackers.

THE KNIFE

Although it is obviously not an effective weapon for keeping attackers at a distance—which is the prime responsibility of the BG—the blade is still worthy of inclusion in the BG's armament. Up front, though, it should be pointed out that the idea of pulling out a secret knife to use after being taken captive is very farfetched. BGs are hyperexpendable; they are normally hit hard and fast in an attempt to take them out immediately. A live diplomat or businessman may be

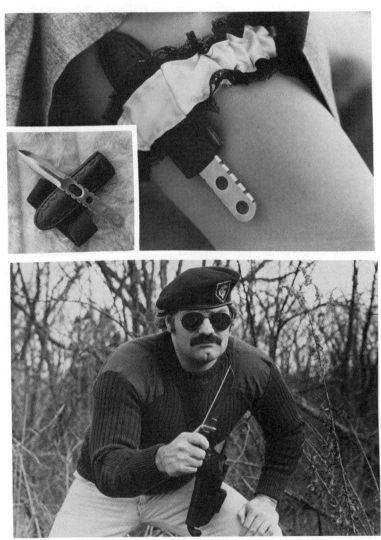

Cold Steel's Urban Shiv conceals well, making it a good choice for the bodyguard. See the ministiletto in the inset. Women can use the garter carry shown above, while men can wear it on an arm or leg. A piercing point on the Tanto below makes it a good blade for paramilitary use.

worth a ransom or have propaganda value to the attackers, but a live BG is only a threat.

The knife's real value is for silent use at close quarters when the show or sound of a gun would be undesirable. I once used my blade to slit the belt of a particularly obnoxious paparazzo who had been annoying a client. The photographer's trousers were then yanked down around his knees. By the time he had recovered his composure and re-covered his posterior, the client had left the scene, and I had blended into the crowd. It should be noted that in this situation, I had been working from within the crowd while two associates handled the close-in protection. As a result, the paparazzo didn't even know, though he no doubt had suspicions, that it was a member of the security team who had dealt with him. More than one BG, by the way, has been offered substantial sums to eliminate members of the sensationalist press such as the paparazzi. I have, in fact, destroyed the film in a few cameras when a photograph could have compromised my identity. That was, of course, in the days before I began decorating books and magazine articles with my mug.

One BG who has worked in Pakistan uses the blade a lot because firing a shot in the massed humanity in that country could cause a riot, thus endangering his client more than a potential attacker. He carries a handgun (which he usually buys in Darra as needed), too, but in crowds he prefers to keep a blade handy. A good BG, of course, prefers to keep his client out of crowds, but when guarding an official or a politico, this is often impossible.

When doing estate security or paramilitary, private army work, I often carry a military-style fighting knife, normally a Gerber or a Fairbairn-Sykes. The latter is carried, by the way, not because I am unaware of the F-S's tendency to snap off at the ricasso but out of affection for the blade. Lately, I have also been using the Tanto, an excellent fighter from

Cold Steel, as my principal fighting knife. This edged weapon offers both a razor-sharp cutting edge and an armor-piercing point, the latter a useful adjunct for either elimination of an opponent or freeing a client from a wrecked chopper or vehicle.

I normally work more covertly, however, in a business suit, and for such times, I choose two compact fighting knives from Cold Steel. The Urban Shiv, a six-and-one-half-inch mini-stiletto, is normally carried in an upside-down sheath on the left arm just inside the coat sleeve. This allows an easy, right-hand draw. Another Cold Steel blade, the Urban Skinner, a four-and-five-eighths-inch push dagger, is also carried somewhere on the person. The Bali-Song butterfly knife is also occasionally carried.

If all of this talk of weapons seems paranoid, remember that the BG is, by definition, a professional paranoid. His job is to assume that someone is out to get his employer. Remember, too, that any weapon, no matter how good it is, is simply an object. It is the *wielder* of the weapon who makes it an effective offensive or defensive tool, or an ineffective one. Weapons choice is important, but time spent mastering the weapon is even more important. Someone more profound than I once said: "Beware the man who owns one gun if he shoots it all of the time."

The evaluation of weapons in this chapter is based on my experiences and the experiences of other pros. These conclusions may disagree with the general "conception" of combat handguns. Remember, however, that these guns are not being considered for competition shooting, police work, or military issue, but for use by a BG, especially one who works in business clothing. Whatever weapons a BG chooses, if he's a real pro, he will find the time to become highly competent in their usage.

4. VEHICULAR SECURITY

THE PROTECTEE IS HIGHLY VULNER-able while traveling between such relatively secure havens as his home and office. Eighty percent of terrorist kidnappings, for example, take place while the target is traveling in an automobile. A high percentage of assassinations also take place while the victim is in a motor vehicle. Just to name a few of the more prominent, Archduke Francis Ferdinand, King Alexander I of Yugoslavia, Pancho Villa, John F. Kennedy, Anastasio Somoza, and Rafael Trujillo were all killed while in automobiles.

Because the danger while traveling in an automobile is so great, the BG must give special attention to the problem of vehicular security. Routes should be varied whenever possible to avoid establishing a pattern that would allow an ambush to be planned. Traffic jams should be avoided since they can immobilize the vehicle, allowing an easy attack. Superhighways, motorways, or other "express" routes are normally preferable. If possible and the manpower is available, routes should be reconned in advance to spot potential trouble areas. Locations of traffic lights, one-way streets, sharp turns, and tall buildings which might house snipers should all be noted. Limousines are very easy to spot and should be avoided if possible in favor of lower profile transport. Clients may need to purchase a large, heavy-duty, four-wheel drive vehicle such as the Land Rover or Jeep Wagoneer since it attracts less attention and offers the added evasion bonus of off-road capability.

An extensive array of modifications are available for making an automobile more resistant to attack. In the trade this is known as *hardening* the vehicle. The most obvious addition is armor plating, though the old-style heavy steel plate should be avoided because it severely impedes the vehicle's performance, and the ability to evade an attack must remain a prime objective. Lighter Kevlar, aluminum oxide ballistic ceramic tiles, and laminated nylon offer good protection, yet are light enough that the vehicle's performance remains high, especially if a high-performance engine is chosen as it should be. The door panels, trunk, floor, roof, and engine compartment should be hardened. The armored floor is especially important to protect against bombs, grenades, and mines detonated beneath the vehicle. Windows should be of layered bullet- and blast-resistant glass. Tinted windows are also advantageous to guard the privacy of the vehicle's occupant and to prevent attackers from readily spotting his or her exact location within the vehicle.

"Run-flat," compartmentalized, self-sealing tires which can be driven on at high speeds even after receiving multiple punctures should be installed, as should fuel cells that retard the possibility of fire if punctured. Another very important defensive measure is the installation of reinforced bumpers on both the front and rear of the car. This will allow for ramming other vehicles attempting to block or halt the protectee's car. In many cases, ramming the rear or front of a block car is far more effective than the bootlegger's turn or the other, more showy evasive maneuvers. Most experts believe, in fact, that had Aldo Moro's driver rammed his attackers, Moro would have escaped.

In addition to these basic measures, more exotic systems can be added making the vehicle something out of a James Bond movie. The ability to lay oil slicks, smoke screens, or caltrops can be incorporated, for example. Lights can also be

The personal bodyguard may help check the limo for explosive devices, although the bodyguard should not do double duty as the driver. A highly polished vehicle is not only attractive, but it also shows telltale marks and fingerprints resulting from tampering.

effectively utilized for defense. High-intensity lights mounted on the rear of the vehicle can blind pursuers at night, while a strobe can disrupt a sniper's aim. Lack of lights can also be used by incorporating night vision devices so that the driver can navigate without head lamps. To defend against hostile crowds, tear gas dispensers can be incorporated, and the lower body moldings of the vehicle can be given razor-sharp edges so that they cannot be grabbed to tip the vehicle over. I have heard of at least one vehicle designed so that an electrical charge can be sent through the exterior of the vehicle. To avoid gas attack or for use in an environment filled with CS gas (e.g. driving through a riot), a completely closed air conditioning system can also be incorporated into the vehicle.

For more aggressive defense, gun ports or built-in machine guns, shotguns, grenade launchers, etc. can also be added. If the threat is there and the money is available, a very sophisticated vehicle can be constructed.

To effectively use such a rolling fortress, however, requires a well-trained driver. The driver should be skilled in high-speed evasive driving techniques, which will include the bootlegger's turn, J-turn, ramming, countering attempts to run the vehicle off of the road, etc. The good driver will be an expert at evasive driving, but will also—if necessary—be able to use the vehicle as a weapon. Secondly, the driver should be skilled with the SMG and the handgun. It should be noted, however, that I am emphatically against the practice of the driver being the sole BG. His job is to drive. The minimum security team in a vehicle should consist of the driver and one BG riding shotgun. The BG will take care of getting the protectee down on the floor under cover, handle any gunplay, and act as the "navigator" and spotter for the driver while he gets the vehicle away from the trouble. Generally, in simplest terms, the driver should concentrate on getting the vehicle away from the scene of trouble as fast as possible. With few exceptions, movement is a primary defense. The driver should also know the best route to the nearest hospital and police station should these facilities be needed.

Many pros feel the best system is to use two or even three cars. If multiple cars are used, the lead car usually contains security men and serves as a scout for the protectee's car. If a third car is used, it is a "trailer" behind the protectee's car. If two cars are used, the second car can act as a trailer to shut off pursuit or to block off an entrance to an area after the VIP car has entered. In addition to offering more fire-power, multiple cars allow for a pick-up of the protectee if his car is disabled.

Bombs are another real threat to vehicles. Some automobiles are even equipped with remote control ignitions so that they can be started without anyone in the car. Others have jamming devices which disrupt radio-controlled bombs. Of the basic types of fuses for explosive devices—chemical, electrical, flame or heat, and mechanical—all can be used on automobiles.

All vehicles used by the protectee should be parked in secure areas and should be equipped with alarm systems which will be set-off by tampering. Still, the driver may need to go through a complete check procedure after the vehicle has been sitting. The following steps will normally suffice if good vehicle security has been followed:

1. If possible go around the vehicle with either a sniffer dog, which will normally go into a "sit" if there are explosives present, or a mechanical bomb sniffer. A well-trained dog can detect TNT, plastic explosives (C3, C4, Cyclonite), gun-cotton, picric acid (TNP), or the Nitroglycerin explosives (gelignite, dynamite, etc.). Dogs, however, cannot detect explosives they have not been trained to "sniff" for. Mechanical sniffers are normally not as efficient as dogs, and they suffer

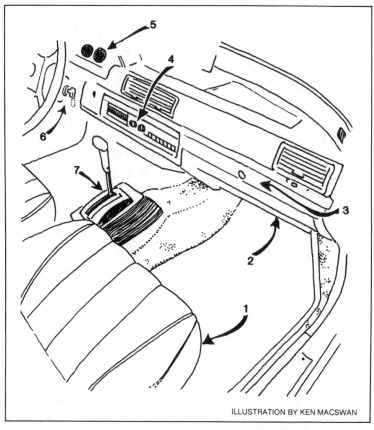

ILLUSTRATION BY KEN MACSWAN

After making certain the doors are not bobby-trapped, the interior of a vehicle should be carefully checked. Look under the seats (1) with a mirror for pressure-sensitive devices and beneath the dash (2) for odd wires. Check for tampering of the glovebox (3), radio or tape deck (4), and gear shift (7). The ignition (6) is the most likely point of tampering, along with the speedometer (5), since a type of delay fusing can be attached.

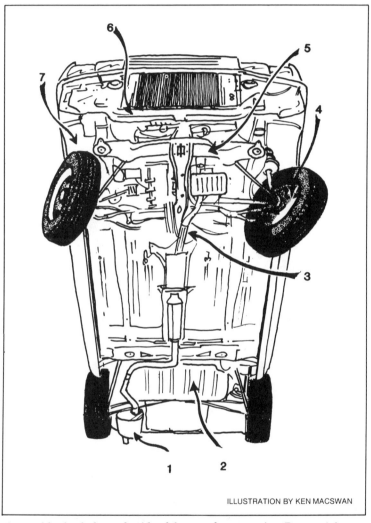

ILLUSTRATION BY KEN MACSWAN

Thoroughly check the underside of the auto for tampering. Pay special attention to the muffler (1) and tail pipes, looking for blockage. Check the fuel tank (2) for explosives and the drive shaft (3) for a fusing device. Wheels and brakes (4) should be examined for devices, along with the frame (5). Look at the radiator (6) for heat-sensitive fuses. Search the wheel wells (7).

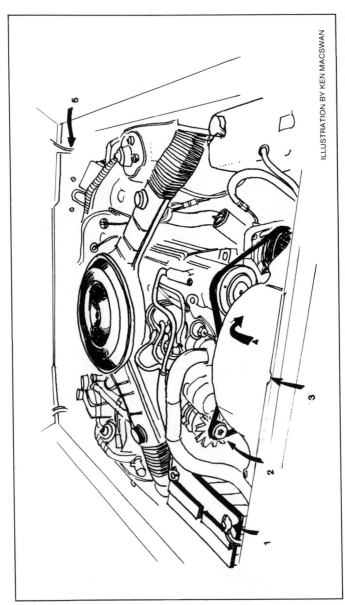

ILLUSTRATION BY KEN MACSWAN

Make sure that no trip wires have been attached to the springs (5) or latch (3) before checking under the hood. Special attention should be paid to the battery and its cables (1) for stray wires. The fan belt and other belts (2) should be checked for detonating devices. Look for heat-sensitive devices on the radiator (4).

from some of the same disadvantages. They are normally dependent on the presence of vapors. No "sniffer" should be considered foolproof, especially if one is dealing with an assassin who is expert in explosives. Note: Other explosives likely to be encountered are Tetryl, PETN (including Primacord or detonating cord), and Amatol.

2. Walk around the vehicle looking for anything that seems out of the ordinary—grease spots on a clean car, handprints on a dirty car, pieces of wire, grease spots on the ground, etc. Do not touch the car. Walk around again looking closely for scratches around doors, windows, hood, trunk, and elsewhere. Look for protruding wires or fingerprints.

3. Look within wheel wells and in areas visible from the access point. Especially observe the shock absorbers to make sure nothing has been attached and observe the brake lines, if visible, for tampering.

4. Using an illuminated inspection mirror such as the Allen Type VM, check beneath the vehicle. Especially check exhaust pipes and muffler, axles, underside of engine, frame, gas tank, transmission, drive shaft, etc. Look not only for an obvious explosive device but also for any sign of tampering, such as a clean area, or anything else suspicious.

5. Look inside the vehicle for signs of tampering such as loose wires, stains on the seats, or anything out of the ordinary. Look especially for any wires leading to doors.

6. Open each door but leave each latched on the safety latches. Run some thin object such as a credit card or thin ruler slowly around the edge of the door to check for wires. Do this for each door, opening each one as it is completed. Do not, however, enter the car or touch anything on the interior.

7. Once all doors are open, check the interior visually and with either a canine or mechanical sniffer if available. Also make use of one's own olfactory powers by being alert

to the smell of bitter almond or any other odd odor. Cover-up odors such as aerosol spray or perfume should also be suspect. Pressure detonators have been fitted so that sitting on the front or rear seat trips them; hence, avoid putting any pressure on the seats. Using an inspection mirror check under seats, under dash, etc. Also check ashtrays, glove compartment, etc., remaining alert for trip wires.

8. Pop the hood but leave on the safety latch. Once again run a credit card or thin object around, slowly checking for trip wires. When satisfied, lift the hood and check the engine, battery, radiator (heat sensitive detonators have been attached to the radiator), master cylinder, and fan belts (trip wires have also been attached to flywheels). Remain alert for anything that appears suspicious. Obviously, reasonable knowledge of what should be under the hood of a car is imperative. Note: Some experts believe the engine compartment should be checked early and the battery cables disconnected to deprive any explosive device of electricity while checking the remainder of the vehicle.

9. Pop the trunk lid but leave it on safety latch. Check the edges as with the hood. Then lift the trunk lid and check the interior thoroughly. It may be necessary to remove the spare tire to check under it. Because of its proximity to the gas tank on many types of automobiles, the trunk has been used to hide incendiaries, and careful attention should be given to looking for same.

10. Start the vehicle—by remote control if possible. Note: No two-way radios should be used near the vehicle during the check procedure.

Obviously, a thorough check is a time-consuming process, and once a vehicle has been checked, it should be kept secure. A driver who understands the need to keep an eye (preferably both of them) on the vehicle 100 percent of the time is a must. So are vehicle alarms on the doors, hood, and trunk. An alarm sensitive to movement may also be useful, even an ultrasonic one sensitive to movement within a few feet of the vehicle would be justified unless the car is parked on a heavily traveled street. The hood and gas cap should be fitted with locks as should the doors and the trunk. When the vehicle is serviced, the driver should, if at all possible, stay with it and watch the mechanics. If not possible, a complete vehicle check should be run after servicing.

When the protectee has been dropped off at his destination, the driver should park the vehicle so that it is not blocked in. A getaway route should always be available. Normally, it is better to back into a parking space. If the situation is a high-threat one, the driver should be in the vehicle with the engine running. In any case, the driver should know when the protectee is about to exit a building to enter the vehicle so he can have it started and ready to move out in an emergency.

Getting the protectee to and from the vehicle is also an operation which must be carried out carefully. The vehicle should be parked as close to the building as possible, with the rear door in line with the entrance to the building. This leaves the shortest distance for the protectee to travel while he's exposed and at least partially shields him with the vehicle. In leaving a building, the BG should exit first, proceed to the vehicle, and open the door with his nongun hand. During this process, the BG must remain extremely alert to potential threats. In getting from the vehicle to the building, the BG should proceed to the building, opening the door with his nongun hand.

When the protectee, chauffeur, and one BG are in the car, the protectee will usually sit behind the BG. If two BGs plus the driver are on duty, the second sits in the back seat behind the driver. If two BGs are escorting the protectee into the building, they will normally position themselves slightly behind and to the sides of the protectee so that he is shielded from the street by their bodies. Upon reaching the entrance, one will move ahead to get the door. He may then remain on duty there or follow, depending upon the situation. A two-man drill leaving the building reverses this procedure, with the BGs moving in front of the protectee and slightly to the sides.

Many experts consider a three- or four-man team the optimum for foot escort. In the case of a three-man team, they form a V either in front of or behind the protectee, depending on whether the building is being entered or exited. A four-man team forms a triangle.

Whichever foot-escort technique is used to get the protectee to or from the vehicle, however, it is important to move quickly between the building and the vehicle and to keep alert to the possibility of attack from all angles, including from above when tall buildings are near. Obviously, this can be a very difficult operation for the lone BG.

Vehicular security is complex and requires a reasonable amount of expertise and experience. That's one reason why a specialist driver is important. He can concentrate on his job knowing that another BG is available to help identify threats and take action to counter them. The primary BG, knowing a trained driver is behind the wheel, can concentrate on getting the protectee between the vehicle and the buildings and on dealing with external threats.

Security for aircraft, boats, trains, and other types of transport involves additional expertise and, normally, additional manpower. Ex-SEALs, for example, may be hired to check yacht hulls for explosives and to provide security while at sea. The Secret Service has developed an entire drill for checking presidential aircraft, even making sure that nothing has been done to structurally weaken a helicopter's rotor blades or a fixed wing aircraft's wings. The complexity of a protectee's private transport fleet and the magnitude of the

A dog trained in explosives detection can be very helpful in checking dwellings or autos for incendiaries.

threat he faces will dictate the measures which must be taken to protect him in the air and at sea.

It should be remembered, however, that an aircraft is especially vulnerable to being mechanically disabled, thus indicating that a twenty-four-hour armed guard may be necessary in the hangar. Note also that the isolation at sea makes a yacht potentially dangerous as well. In some parts of the world, piracy is still a threat, and I have been hired on numerous occasions for cruises specifically to counter modern Captain Kidds. As a result, at least a reasonable portion of the crew of a VIP's yacht should be trained with weapons (ex-SEALs, Incursori, SBS, etc. are especially good), and a twenty-four-hour armed guard should be mounted at all times aboard the vessel. When in port, while the protectee is aboard, or when in a high-threat area at sea, a BG should supplement the armed crewman.

The primary focus of this chapter is protection when automobiles are in use but many of the same procedures may apply when moving between a helicopter and a vehicle or in other situations.

5. HIGH-PROFILE, LOW-PROFILE BODYGUARD

IT IS A FACT OF LIFE (OR PERHAPS death) that the BG is highly expendable. Any terrorist or kidnapper who gives any thought to an attack on a target protected by one or more BGs realizes that the elimination of those protectorates at the earliest possible moment is highly desirable. As a result, it is to the BG's advantage to be as unobtrusive as possible, thus making it more difficult to identify him. This blending into the background is what is usually known as operating *low profile*.

Many employers, especially executives or government officials who must carry out their everyday duties while being guarded, prefer low-profile BGs in any case. To blend into the milieu a protectee moves in, the executive-level BG must dress and act as part of the client's normal entourage, yet must be ready to go into action instantly. This means, for example, that if the BG is carrying a briefcase, it should remain in the "weak" hand so that the gun hand is always free for the draw. If right-handed, ex-military officers do this instinctively, having been trained to carry a briefcase in the left hand to keep the right hand free for saluting. Following the waste-not-want-not precept, many BGs who need to carry a briefcase to blend in, use it as a receptacle for a SMG.

When working low-profile, one must always attempt to position himself between the employer and the most likely threat area without being obvious. Likewise, excuses which seem mundane should be made for doing things dictated by security. Whenever possible, for example, an excuse should be found for drawing blinds or drapes so that a sniper cannot readily identify a target. A well-trained client will often give such an excuse by complaining of the brightness from outside. If possible, the BG should work with his employer's secretary so that meeting rooms are set up in advance to enable the employer and the BG to be positioned facing the door with backs to a wall. That is, of course, assuming that the BG is operating with a cover that will allow him to accompany his client into meetings.

If posing as some type of junior executive or civil servant to justify accompanying his employer, one should do enough homework so that if he is asked a question concerning his supposed job, a reasonably intelligent answer can be given. One BG, a former stockbroker and former member of 21SAS, gave such good financial advice to one of his protectees that he was offered an executive position in financial management. Fortunately for the average BG, junior factotums are usually expected to be seen rather than heard.

One does not want to be obviously seen, however, and dress is extremely important. Many BGs in the United States are off-duty police officers who, even though they wear a coat and tie, look exactly like off-duty police officers. If one wants to command top pay as a BG he has to be willing to dress the part. This will normally mean in conservative, well-cut business suits. John T. Molloy's *Dress for Success* might be worth reading since many executives consider it their guidebook for attire. The BG, of course, has the added disadvantage of having to conceal one or more pieces of lethal hardware about his person. This means that custom-tailored

The bodyguard here secures a stairway before his protectee comes down, while another bodyguard secures the opposite side. Each has his back protected and can check his partner's blind area. Once the area is considered secure, each bodyguard will move to the bottom of the stairs and position himself against the wall to cover all areas except above. The chauffeur will cover that area while holding the door open.

suits are in order. It's a comment on English sartorial poise that my London tailor has never asked the reason for cutting my suits to fit over a brace of handguns.

If one carries a fairly heavy weapon on the belt, slightly oversize belt loops are an advantage so that a fairly thick gun belt (though trophy buckles or anything else "cowboy" should be avoided unless one is an ex-Texas Ranger working out of Dallas) can be worn to distribute the weight and avoid sagging trousers. If custom-made by a holster maker who understands what is required, even a one-inch gun belt, if well-designed, can suffice. Suspenders may also be useful to help support the weight of a fully loaded handgun.

I have found—though this may be purely subjective—that conservative pin-striped suits tend to conceal firearms better. For some reason, the vertical stripes distract a viewer from noticing any slight bulge should movement tighten the coat for an instant. Whenever possible, of course, the coat should be worn unbuttoned for faster access to the weapon.

One subtlety some BGs engage in when working low profile yet still wanting to flash a low-key signal to any other BGs is the use of the "regimental" tie. Only someone at close quarters will spot it and often only a pro will recognize it. More than once I have been working a social function and spotted a subtle blue SAS regimental tie or a Foreign Legion paratroop tie on another BG. Usually that same individual notes my Society of Vietnamese Rangers tie and draws the same conclusion. Normally, one knows who the other BGs are but not always, and it can be life-or-death to know who *not* to drop if they show a firearm. Of course, no pro is going to assume someone is all right just because of his tie. No pro, in fact, will assume someone is all right even if he flashes the most official-looking ID the BG has ever seen. Suspicion is an occupational necessity for the BG. The tie, the SOG Association pin, or some other subtle tip-off can at least alert

A bodyguard must be able to get his well-concealed weapon quickly into action. The tie shown at top is from the Society of Vietnamese Rangers and is a subtle signal to other guards that this man is a good guy. Suits should be custom-tailored to fit over handguns with minimum show. Well-cut clothing is essential for the bodyguard working low profile.

the BG about who to check on as potential allies.

Speaking of social functions, the BG may have to be able to blend into some fairly sophisticated social situations. I have been hired for more than one job because I was at a "good university" rather than because I could shoot straight. The old cliches from the James Bond movies about knowing the proper fork to lift and which wine to drink with which course may truly be of importance if one is working low profile and has to blend in at social functions. Once again, because of the "tea battles" one undergoes in officer's training, a commissioned military background will give at least a veneer of social polish. I have also found that having a good knowledge of literature, art, music, drama, and film has stood me in good stead at various social functions when I was trying to blend in with the guests. On the other hand, my abysmal ignorance about race horses, trendy discos, and jet set boutiques has caused me to be thought out of touch with "reality." Lest all this talk of jet set socializing be misinterpreted, it should be noted, however, that for every social event where the BG mills with the guests, there will be ten where he stands guard in drafty halls or sits watching the limo. Still, the "numero uno" BG for a truly high-threat target, will usually stay close to his protectee, and that's when the social graces, combined with ability to deal with those practicing the antisocial graces, can mean double the salary.

Being polyglot is almost essential, too, if one works outside the USA. English, French, German, Spanish, Italian, Arabic, and Mandarin Chinese are all very useful languages for the BG, though unless one is really good at languages, reasonable fluency in one or two languages in addition to one's native tongue is about all that can be hoped for. Fortunately, English is spoken in most parts of the world so I have managed to get by with English, German, and a smattering of Mandarin Chinese, although I am working on Spanish and French as well. Often, English and French will get one by in the Middle East, but the BG who has other good credentials and can speak Arabic—one real advantage held by many ex-members of the SAS—has a real edge in finding jobs in that volatile part of the world where good BGs are always in demand.

No matter how well one operates in low profile, he may be spotted. An Italian fashion designer once spotted my shoulder rig even under a well-cut coat fitted to the rig. Clothes were her profession. I have also been frequently spotted by other security pros, but that's their job. Once a potential assassin was arrested with my photograph indicating that a hit on the protectee was being contemplated, and that I was being identified for removal.

Perhaps the biggest advantage of blending into the milieu is that the BG does not become an annoyance to his employer. This means one can do the job more efficiently by remaining close to the employer in case of trouble. Sometimes this works in odd situations. I once found myself completely accepted into the household of a client who had a reputation for chewing up BGs for breakfast and for having a low tolerance for their presence. As it happened, the client was a rare book collector, and I had worked for a rare book dealer at one time. The BG has to learn not to "hover"—not to crowd his employer's space—yet to be ready to move in to prevent trouble.

Most of the discussion of low-profile operations so far has stressed formal occasions, but it is sometimes even more difficult to remain low profile in informal situations. The BG, for example, has problems if his employer is a nudist, a dilemma once supposedly faced by a man guarding a movie star, though the story was told over a few pints and may have grown with the telling. In actuality, the BG who overcame his or her modesty would find that a nudists' gathering would be perfect since it would be instantly obvious if anyone were armed. The rub (no pun intended) would come, however, when the BG had to decide where to carry his armament.

It behooves the BG who is likely to work in informal situations to find sports clothes which will also conceal firearms. I once had a yachting cap rigged with a holster for a .25 Browning and used it more than once. Golf bags are great for carrying SMGs and chopped-down shotguns, but the open spaces on golf courses also are inviting to snipers. When guarding a client who likes to ski, the BG also needs to be a competent skier, not only to blend in but to keep up. An Austrian female BG I knew grew up on skis and could also shoot very, very straight. During the ski season, she operated almost entirely guarding people on the slopes and used to work the skiing areas of Lebanon. She looked so good in ski pants that she was not low profile, but she was hard to spot as a BG. When asked what she did for a living, she used to reply that she was a securities salesperson. The latter was, of course, a pun. Although she normally carried a .380 PPK, for the longer ranges likely to be encountered protecting skiers, she used a SIG 9mm carried in a parka pocket.

At the completely opposite end of the spectrum is the BG who is meant to be a threat and, as a result, works extremely high profile. Perhaps the best example of this is the Hell's Angel who guards a rock star. No one is in doubt who or what he is, but he is not intended to counter a professional assassin; he deals with groupies or deranged fans. As a result, the reputation of a biker makes him a good choice.

Often an estate will be guarded by fairly high-profile security people who are meant to intimidate anyone contemplating breaking in. Some type of uniform and an aggressive show of firepower, dogs, electronic hardware, etc. is called for in this situation. In some third world countries, the BG is meant to be seen as an ostentatious flaunting of the employer's power. As a result, cammies and berets, along with SMGs, are obviously displayed, and the security force is often run on paramilitary lines. I once served with a six-man team on such an assignment, and everyone even wore their military qualifications badges as part of the dog and pony show. Jump wings from all over the world were on display, offering any sniper who wanted to eliminate members of this formidable-looking crew an easy aiming point. All were well-qualified to "kick ass and take names," too, assuming those hypothetical snipers, who could spot them very easily, were not around to eliminate them at the start of hostilities. Another time, I carried a nickeled Model 59 S&W with pearl grips very openly because my employer wanted it known he was guarded by an armed BG. It should be noted, by the way, that I also had a S&W Model 38 which I would have used through the pocket of my bush jacket while someone was watching the shiny 59.

Normally, the BG will find that he sometimes works low profile and sometimes high profile. Often, one will have to operate in a high-profile mode some of the time and in a low-profile mode the rest of the time on the same job. Occasionally, one will also operate high profile as a "stalking horse" intended to be obvious, while someone else operating low profile is the back-up.

One of the most pleasant jobs I even had was guarding a rather congenial group aboard a large ocean-going yacht cruising the Mediterranean Sea. While at sea, I normally wore trunks and an obvious shoulder rig (in case of "pirates") since everyone on board knew who I was anyway. When the yacht was in port and I was guarding it, I kept the hardware hidden but obviously patrolled the boat as a deterrent to theft. If it was necessary to accompany any of the party ashore, then I operated in a low profile mode.

In this case, the yacht had one crewman who was a former "Marine Commando" in his country's armed forces

ILLUSTRATION BY KEN MACSWAN

Here is a perfect example of a "high-profile" bodyguard.

and who normally guarded the yacht. While I was ashore, he took over the security of the vessel. In some of the ports, I could not legally carry firearms ashore, but the party did not really fear assassination as much as robbery or hassles by the "peasants," so I felt relatively confident with two blades in lieu of the gun. Occasionally, even where it was banned, I may have forgotten to take the .25 Browning out of my cap, however.

One of the hazards of working low profile is that one may get so wrapped up in being part of the surroundings that he forgets why he is there. More than once, I was guarding someone at a social gathering and had to remind myself that I was there to watch doors, windows, and suspicious-looking guests (which at some gatherings pretty well takes in everyone) rather than well-formed ladies in low-cut gowns. Speaking of low-cut gowns, I once worked a high-profile job in which I frisked everyone who entered my employer's presence— male or female. Great diplomacy and deftness of touch were required, but since everyone already knew what to expect, no problems were encountered.

When a BG consistently works high profile, he may find himself adopting affectations to look meaner: a shaved head or Fu Manchu moustache may seem to enhance one's "steely-eyed killer" look. Large physical size can be a real advantage to a BG who works entirely in situations where he is meant to present an obvious threat. Many professionals call such BGs "Oddjobs" from the movie Goldfinger or "Tiger Men" from the Buck Rogers series and don't consider them particularly effective against major-league opposition. In reality, it depends on the individual. I know high-profile BGs who are big, ugly, tough, and competent to handle any situation that arises. An equal number, however, are just big and ugly and wouldn't last long against a "shooter." A BG who is big enough and mean-looking enough to deter low-level threats (i.e. irate former employees of the client, drunks, muggers, etc.), yet not so large or outlandish-looking to draw attention is normally the best compromise.

Although there are no hard and fast rules, the BG who can move in sophisticated circles undoubtedly will command a much higher salary than one who can work only in the high-visibility, deterrent jobs. The average rock star, for example (with the exception of a few British ones guarded by the same competent ex-SAS men who snatched one of the Great Train Robbers away from his sanctuary in Latin America), hires his BGs by the dozen, or by the ton, and pays them accordingly. A dozen muscular karate instructors may keep unwanted guests out, but they won't stop professional assassins or kidnappers. It takes a pro to counter a pro, and the client who is truly in a high-threat situation realizes this and is willing to pay accordingly. If not, he often learns the error of his ways in the ultimate manner. His successor usually hires a pro.

6. AREA SECURITY

PROVIDING AREA SECURITY IS ONE OF the BG's most important jobs, yet it is frequently neglected. In its broadest terms, area security should provide a perimeter defense which will halt low- to medium-level threats and give warning of penetrating high-level threats so that counter-measures can be taken. The effectiveness of area security is highly dependent upon manpower, hardware, and the location to be secured. Generally, most effective area security systems rely on *defense in-depth*. As each layer of a defense in-depth is penetrated, an attacker theoretically meets stiffer and stiffer opposition until he is stopped short of the target.

Since the protectee probably spends more time at his residence, and since his home should be his safe refuge, great care should be taken in planning the defenses surrounding a residence. An estate in which the dwelling is surrounded by grounds is easier to secure than an apartment or a town house, but it also requires more manpower and more hardware.

The first step in any area security system is establishing what is known as *access control*. Controlled access limits entry to certain points where anyone attempting to pass through must undergo scrutiny before being admitted. Such scrutiny can be performed by an armed guard or a CCTV (closed circuit television) system. A combination of the two may be the most effective. The area should also be surrounded by some type of barrier which inhibits intruders and channels legitimate visitors to the access point. On an estate, this barrier

83

may be a brick, stone, or chain link fence. The fence should be topped by barbed wire and barbed tape to discourage climbers.

Normally, the primary advantage of a chain link fence is that it grants an intruder no place to hide, especially if undergrowth, trees, etc. are cleared within a reasonable distance of the fence. The chain link fence also allows patrolling guards to see an intruder. The disadvantage of the chain link fence is that it is less attractive than a solid fence and gives less privacy. An intruder can also see where the guards are through a chain link fence and observe what's going on inside. A security lighting system aimed at the chain link fence can, however, eliminate this problem by blinding anyone trying to see inside. Two fences are useful. They should be spaced far enough apart so that jumping from one to the other is impossible. The outer fence should be stone or brick topped with barbed wire, while the inner one should be a chain link. This ensures privacy from the outside, but also allows guards to see anyone between the fences from inside the perimeter.

Security lights should be used at night inside the inner fence facing outward. They should be positioned so that there are no dead zones and so they shine outward, illuminating an area up to twenty-five yards outside the fence or, in the case of a double fence, illuminating the area up to the solid fence. This system blinds any intruder and keeps him from identifying the location of patrolling security personnel. It also allows the patrolling guards, who will be in darkness, to retain some of their night vision.

Moving searchlights, though used in prison movies, are a poor choice for security. Anyone trained in incursion tactics has learned the old dictum: freeze when the light moves, and move when it stops.

Since the primary purpose of the perimeter is to either discourage an intruder, or barring that, to warn of the intrusion, various types of sensors can be used in conjunction with the fences. Hung directly on the fence, for example, can be vibration sensors, electrical or magnetic fields protection, or low-frequency audio scanners. Fence-mounted detectors are useful for warning of attempts to scale the fence, but they can also be set off by high winds. Use of what is known as an accumulator can lessen the chances of the wind setting off a vibration or other fence-mounted detector. Free-standing sensors can include beam-breakage microwave scanners, photo-electric beams (either used singly or stacked in multiples), electro-magnetic volume protection, buried seismic detectors, or video motion detectors. Multiple systems are usually best, and many companies such as Aritech offer systems which operate with various types of sensors. Seismic sensors are very good but can be set off by mistake in any well-traveled area. They are most useful seeded around some highly vulnerable area such as a final alarm before it is penetrated.

One of my favorite systems is the beam-breaking microwave scanner, especially some of those available from Southwest Microwave. There is even a solar-powered model—the 300B—which is in wide use in the Middle East. This video motion detector is good since it can be combined with a surveillance camera which scans a section of fence. The video motion detector works on a principle of comparison as the system checks the scene being photographed against the one shortly before and reacts to sharp changes in brightness and contrast. If photo-electric beams are used, they should be stacked so they cannot be avoided. Intrusion detection systems should also be zoned so that the area of the intrusion can be pinpointed immediately. When the area being protected is isolated, spare parts for all critical security systems should be maintained and a back-up power system should be available.

For access through the PM (perimeter), there must be a

The Model 300 Microwave Intrusion Link in place at top is portable and can be used outdoors and inside in certain situations. The 300A Model from Southwest Microwave shown in the inset gives up to 500 feet of protection per link. Useful in third world countries with little electricity but plenty of sun is the Model 300B Microwave Intrusion Link shown below, which is solar-powered.

gate or gates. Two gates are preferred to allow a point of escape for the protectee in a worst-case scenario. Traditionally, gates have been manned by security personnel, which is still a good system if manpower is not limited. When manpower is limited, however, a system in which callers at a gate are monitored by a CCTV can be set up. Admission can be via remote control or a mobile security vehicle can arrive to open the gate either manually or remotely after double checking the person or persons desiring admittance. If a guardhouse is located at the gate, it should have hardened walls and glass to defend against attack and a back-up CCTV monitor in case of an assault on the gate. A two-way communications system should be maintained between the gatehouse and the security control center, which will normally be in the residence.

In one estate system I designed for a very high-risk target who had had multiple attempts made on his life for political reasons, I used CCTVs with remote control locks on the gates. However, once a vehicle had gained entry, it still had to approach the house via a winding drive. At one point the vehicle was channeled to an avoidable second barricade lined with ditches on the sides of the drive. The vehicle was forced to stop at this point until a mobile security patrol arrived to clear the vehicle through. A sniper armed with a .357 H&H rifle loaded with "solids" which will stop an elephant and penetrate even hardened glass and most armor covered the drive until the vehicle was cleared past this point. At night the rifle bore a starlight scope, and the barricade was situated so that the driver presented an optimum target.

Within the perimeter fencing and intrusion detection screen, the estate should be patrolled if it is reasonably large. For an estate with grounds of ten acres or more, a minimum of one two-man patrol with a dog or, preferably, two two-man patrols with dogs should be used. On smaller estates one two-man patrol team with a dog will suffice. The dog handler should be armed with a handgun and, in high-threat situations, a compact SMG such as the Beretta M12, H&K MP5, etc., while the second man is armed with a handgun and shotgun. Where the SMG is not legal, a large-magazine auto pistol will usually suffice for the dog handler. Additional back-up men should be available to reinforce the patrol team in case of serious attack or the discovery of intruders; a jeep with an M60 mounted is not unheard of for such use. A reserve to throw up a screen around the residence must, of course, be maintained.

An interesting innovation which can be used to supplement a small protective force is the robot designed for PM patrol. Such robots can be used to investigate an intrusion with their mobile cameras and sensors. Though the robots available for industrial security normally have only nonlethal defensive systems such as sirens, bright lights, etc., robots with lethal weapons systems are in use in at least one installation I know of. The robots cannot replace human guards, but they can investigate intrusions without endangering personnel. Many patrol robots are also equipped with heat and smoke sensors and fire fighting equipment so that they can function in the dual role of intrusion and fire security.

The residence itself should have its own intrusion detectors, and doors and windows should be kept locked as much as possible without turning the residence into a prison. Very attractive grates which serve the dual purpose of ornamentation and security for windows and doors can be installed. Such grates should, however, have an internal quick release in case of fire.

Either bullet-resistant glass or ballistic plastic (acrylic or polycarbonite) windows should be installed. The plastic windows are less likely to splinter, although they are more susceptible to scratching. A silicon-based antiabrasive coating greatly increases acrylic's resistance to scratching, however.

A combination of heavy-duty plastic windows internally and bullet-resistant glass windows externally is also a good compromise, offering ballistic protection and giving the same thermal insulation as storm windows. When evaluating glass or plastic for use in "hardening," it is helpful to be acquainted with Underwriter's Laboratory Standard 752 which establishes criteria and ratings for bullet-resistant material. The ratings on different types of "bulletproof" glass or plastic can be checked, and a decision can be made about the level of protection needed. The four standard ratings encountered are:

Medium—Small Arms: resistant to .38 Super Auto
High—Small Arms: resistant to .357 Mag
Super—Small Arms: resistant to .44 Mag
High—Rifle: resistant to .30-06

If needed, glass or plastic resistant to even more powerful weapons can be acquired, but it will have to be special ordered.

It may also be beneficial to paint the exterior walls of the residence with matte white paint since it is virtually impossible to camouflage oneself against this background. Trees around the residence grant both a privacy and antisniper screen. The open "killing zone" should be between the trees and the internal security fence.

The BG must also be prepared to plan for defending a residence which is located on a river, lake, ocean, etc. In this case, underwater security is a consideration, and access from the water must be limited. Barriers such as concrete walls can limit access for swimmers and small boats. Lights on the bottom will also silhouette any swimmer attempting to infiltrate. An extremely expensive proposition—because of the salary of the trainer, the need for special feeding, etc.—would be guard porpoises which are trained to attack intruders. If this seems far fetched, consider that there were dozens of

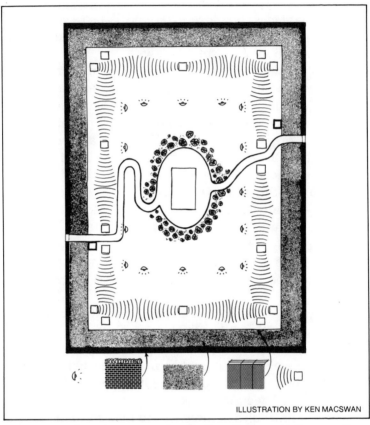

ILLUSTRATION BY KEN MACSWAN

Here is a hypothetical estate security plan for extensive security precautions. The outer wall and inner fence are eight feet high and topped with barbwire. Between the two fences is fine sand, which shows footprints and is covered by microwave sensors. Security lighting is aimed outward. The chain fence forms an L with the brick wall to enclose the area in case dogs are used. Each gate is located in a guard house which controls access. The rear gate, used only for emergency escape, can be opened by remote control. The road curves sharply so that a vehicle is forced to slow down, thereby becoming a target for a sniper. The parklike lawn makes for an effective "killing zone" that gives an intruder no place to hide. Normal security would include two to four gate guards, a sniper in the house, four patrolling guards with dogs, two close-in guards and a guard inside the house manning a command post.

dead VC/NVA combat swimmers in Vietnam whose demise was attributable to the U.S. Navy's attack porpoises. Passive sonar can be used for detection of intruders via water, but it is certainly not 100 percent effective, especially against surface-skimming intruders. Active sonar based on the Doppler principle is probably the most effective for underwater security. Additionally, some type of intrusion-detection sensors should be in place between the water and the residence to act as a backup system to whatever other aquatic intrusion protection is installed.

Securing a town house or apartment from attack is generally much more difficult because there is less area to set up a defense in-depth and because of the need to be less obtrusive about security. In either case, intrusion alarms should be installed on windows and doors. Because the possibilities of a sniper being in a nearby building are much greater, highly bullet-resistant glass or plastic should be installed in windows (rated "High—Rifle" or greater). In a multistory apartment building, the choice of floor is determined by various considerations. A penthouse offers more privacy, for example, but it also requires that much more time be spent on an elevator. An elevator in general use can give a BG nightmares, because it is such a confining space and can easily be sabotaged. If there is a private elevator that can be secured, this problem can be virtually eliminated. In any case, the floor chosen should be high enough that objects thrown from the street, or even a rifle grenade fired from the street, will not reach the residence.

Surveillance cameras should be installed in hallways near the apartment if possible. Generally, there are fewer objections from neighbors than might be expected, since many consider the security precautions deterrents to crime. More than once, when neighbors knew I was in charge of security, they told me they were going out and asked me to keep an eye on their apartments. I gladly provided this service since any "bad guys" getting into a vacant apartment close-by could have been a threat to the protectee. For privacy—both for the protectee and the BG—it is a good idea for the employer to furnish his security personnel with apartments strategically located on the same floor as his. The protectee can then have "panic buttons" installed in his residence so that the BG can be immediately summoned. This system works expecially well with three BGs. One can be on duty at the residence, one off-duty but in his own apartment available for backup, and one off-duty and free to leave. In the case of a town house, live-in BGs should have their rooms located in critical locations such as near the stairs leading to the employer's bedroom. In apartments and town houses, there is always a trade-off between privacy and security, and some system must be worked out which allows the best compromise between the two.

Limiting access as much as possible is important in an apartment building. Again a private elevator is highly desirable but not always available. However, an apartment with a tough doorman and tight restrictions on letting strangers into the building will help. Very healthy tips to the doorman often ensure his loyalty to the protectee so that he immediately lets the BG know if anyone suspicious is around, has been asking questions, etc. In a few third world countries, certain apartment blocks are designed to offer security for foreign businessmen or VIPs, and the doorman himself is a trained security man. Vehicular security is harder to maintain in an apartment building since even the best apartment garages are not 100 percent secure. One with an attendant and/or access from the outside only via a key is desirable. If it's possible to fence or wall the assigned parking space, it should be done.

In both apartments and town houses, it's a good idea for the protectee to have a *saferoom*, a term used in this manual

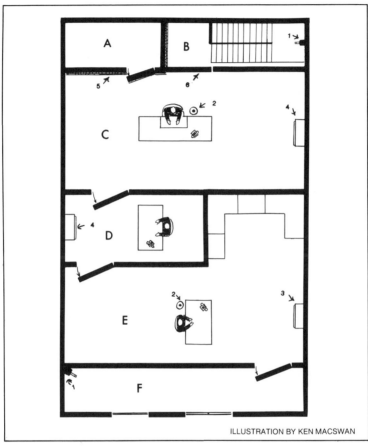

ILLUSTRATION BY KEN MACSWAN

This layout for a high-security office complex shows optimum security precautions. Area F allows access to stairs and elevators and is equipped with a CCTV (1) monitor. Area E is an outer office in which a secretary monitors visitors as they enter Area F. At her left foot is a panic switch (2) to alert the bodyguard and executive which also automatically locks the door between her and Area D, the bodyguard's room. Visitors must pass through Area D, where the guard's camera (4) scans the entrance and emergency exit. Area C, the executive office, is equipped with a panic button (2) and a monitor (4). Area A is a washroom which is also a hardened "saferoom." A hidden door (6) leads to a private stairway and hall, Area B, to the emergency exit.

is a room—often a bathroom—which has "hardened" walls, reinforced door, heavy-duty locks, no windows, emergency medical supplies, a flashlight, secure communications with the outside, and often a weapon. If the protectee is under attack, he and his family can barricade themselves in the saferoom until help arrives, whether it's the BG from down the hall or a roving patrol car summoned by an alarm button.

Special care about who is admitted to an apartment or town house must be taken since there is much less space to slow an attack than there is on an estate with grounds around it. It is even more important to keep one's address a secret. Names on mailboxes and buzzers are not a good idea. The building should be located at the blind end of a dead end street. This makes it much easier to spot cars that are "cruising," since there are fewer valid reasons for vehicles to be approaching. Like the estate, the town house should be painted with matte white paint to silhouette anyone attempting to hide by the house.

When the protectee is away from home, a new group of security considerations must be dealt with in hotels. Many of the same problems which arise in securing an apartment apply to hotel rooms. Again, tips to hall porters, bellboys, desk clerks, elevator operators, doormen, etc. are well-advised so that they pay particular attention to any suspicious persons and let the BG know about them. It is always a good idea for the BG to establish with his employer the need for an expense account specifically used for greasing the tracks or for taking local police liaisons out to dinner. (In some third world countries, the police portion of the budget may include money for bribes as well.)

If the BG is guarding a politico or VIP with enough clout, he should arrange to check out rooftops, offices, etc. overlooking the rooms his protectee will occupy. Except for official government BGs, however, this is rarely practical; hence, it may be necessary to establish a man on top of the hotel to keep an eye on other rooftops and windows. If only one BG is on duty, the best he can do is scan the buildings across the way with day or night glasses as the situation dictates. Heavy curtains should be present in the hotel room so that no one will be silhouetted even against strong interior light.

Entrances and exits to the hotel should all be watched if possible, though this entails a large security staff. As a compromise, all entrances and exits to the protectee's floor can usually be watched by a couple of men. Because hotel lobbies are so busy and are usually located in heavily traveled areas, special attention must be paid to security when entering and leaving the hotel. A team of security men should go ahead and check out the lobby before giving the all-clear, either using radios or the house phone, to bring the protectee down. Small, less ostentatious hotels present less traffic, less staff, and fewer guests to worry about. Even very wealthy clients should forego large luxury hotels for security reasons. Smaller hotels often have only two or three entrances which makes them easier to secure.

It is normally impossible to check out all staff or guests in a hotel; hence, the BG should concentrate on those most likely to come into contact with the protectee. Rooms on either side of the protectee should be occupied by security personnel if possible. If not, the BG should find out who is in these rooms. The rooms directly above and below the protectee's should also be checked since these could also harbor attackers. If the protectee is a politico, any staff member or guest from his home country or from another country likely to harbor a grievance should be checked out and kept away from the protectee. For example, if one were guarding a Turkish businessman, anyone of Armenian descent would have to be considered suspect or likewise if one were guarding a relative of the former Shah of Iran, any Shiite Moslem

A well-trained attack dog, such as this one from SEMO Command School for Dogs, offers excellent area protection, especially when used in conjunction with armed handlers.

would require close scrutiny.

The rooms or suite should be checked for booby traps and explosive devices as well as for "bugs." Some hotels now offer rooms which are RF shielded, making them virtually impervious to eavesdropping. If such rooms are available, the BG should try to obtain them for his client.

Generally, the suite chosen should be on a floor high enough to secure it from ground level (as discussed under apartments), yet not overlooked by other buildings. Preferably, it should be near the end of the corridor to limit traffic. External balconies leading to other rooms or fire escapes should be avoided if possible. Any access door leading to another room or suite should be locked and secured internally. The BG may also want to install some type of portable intrusion alarm system to monitor all doors and windows. A few, but only a very few, hotels geared to VIP guests have suites with alarm systems installed. Assuming the security force is large enough, one BG should remain in the suite at all times, even if the protectee is away. All deliveries to the protectee should also go through the BG.

When eating at the hotel or in other restaurants, try to seat the protectee and his party in a booth or at a table along a wall, but not next to or opposite a window. The table should not be near an entrance or exit. The BG or BGs should be at a table reasonably near the protectee where the protectee's table and the entrances can be observed. It should be arranged with the protectee that the BGs will be allowed to finish eating before he finishes. A tip to the waiter, along with an emphasis on fast service for the BG's table, is a good idea. Frequently, the lone protectee will ask a BG to eat with him for company. In this situation, the BG should seat himself so that he can see anyone approaching the table and so that his draw is not impeded. If the protectee uses a public restroom, a BG should unobtrusively head for the restroom also. Anyone approaching the protectee's table other than the waiter, waitress, busboy, etc. should be watched especially carefully. For that matter, so should the restaurant employees.

Because the sophisticated access controls and intrusion detection systems that can be established at a residence do not exist at a hotel, the BG will have to be particularly alert when guarding his charge in a hotel. It has been my experience that three BGs are the minimum number necessary to adequately protect a client staying in a hotel. Even with three, the defenses are spread thin at times. Probably the best experience I have had with hotels resulted from a client who owned a large interest in a hotel chain. He had a suite designed in each of the hotels he frequented that incorporated all of the security systems I advised. CCTVs monitored the hall, stairway, and elevator on his floor, and intrusion detection systems were installed in the suite. Rooms across the hall and next to the suite were designed as small bedrooms with baths specifically for the security team. Most hotel stays when on protection assignments, however, entail a lot of pressure and little sleep.

How much control the BG has over security at his employer's place of business depends on two basic factors: where the protectee stands in the organization's hierarchy and what type of business he's in. Normally, someone employing a BG is in a relatively high executive position and thus has some control over the security of at least his own office, if not the entire building. Because of corporate spying and counterspying, most industrial or design firms are now much more security conscious, and this works to the BG's advantage. In a firm doing defense contract work, security is usually relatively tight. If the protectee is a relatively high-ranking politico, certain security measures are already in effect in his office building in most countries.

The BG's first concern at the place of business should

be in limiting access. The building should not be one where a person can just walk in off the street and move about without restrictions. A guard at the door should check the identity of all callers, and visitors should be issued a pass that is either taken back before they leave or becomes invalid after one-time use. Some access controls use a punch key system in which each employee has a four- or five-digit entrance code which opens the doors to areas he is cleared for. If the employee is under duress, an additional digit can be punched which still opens the door but also silently alerts the security people.

Direct access to executives likely to be targets should be limited. For example, elevators running to the "executive suites" may need a special card inserted in the control panel to allow travel to that floor. Elevators and stairwells should have surveillance cameras that are monitored from both a guard center and the office of the executive's secretary. Doors to the stairwells should be kept locked so that they cannot be opened from outside, though for safety purposes they can be equipped with panic bars. However, doors should be fitted with an alarm which will sound if opened. All doors to executive offices should be monitored by closed circuit TV cameras as should hallways on the executive floor.

The entrance to the protectee's office should be located across the room from the entrance to the outer/secretary's office, with the secretary's desk located so that she is in between the doors. Her desk should be equipped with a warning button which will alert the protectee, BG, and building guards of attack. This switch should also automatically lock the door leading into the protectee's office. By the way, in some high-protection designs, the BG has an office between that of the secretary and the protectee, and any visitor has to pass through this office on the way in.

Within the executive office should be a hidden door

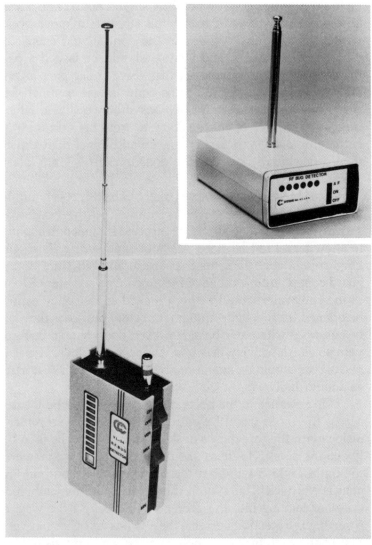

Although the BG's primary concern is not electronic security, compact bug detectors such as the CCS VL34 can be useful. This unit is the size of a cigarette pack. The inset shows the VL33, another compact bug detector.

leading to a secure staircase which can serve as an escape route. It may also be wise to have a "saferoom" with bullet-resistant walls, a reinforced door, and communications equipment. Often, this room can be combined with the private "executive washroom."

It may also be necessary to have certain other areas secure such as executive meeting rooms or an executive dining area. "Panic switches" which instantly send a warning of attack, access control, CCTV, and an armed BG on duty in the area should all be considered.

One other situation which may arise for the BG is protection of his charge at social events, performances, open meetings, or other gatherings at which strangers will be present. Each of these public appearances will present its own problems. In the case of social gatherings (i.e. receptions, parties, fund raisers, etc.), screening guests can be helpful but is not often practical. The use of hand-held metal detectors to check guests is often not practical either, though this method is occasionally used. Normally, the BG or BGs need to be extremely alert, especially to anyone approaching the protectee. I normally work out a signal for the protectee to use if someone is approaching whom he doesn't know.

The BG finds himself in the position of having to remain close enough to react quickly yet far enough away that he doesn't infringe on the protectee's privacy. The BG must also make some effort to blend into the surroundings so undue attention is not drawn to himself. With a male protectee who is not accompanied by his wife, a female BG can remain close at social occasions by being introduced as the protectee's guest. If the protectee is unmarried, no other explanation is normally needed. If, however, the protectee is married, she can be introduced as a distant relative, daughter of an old friend, or friend of his wife's to halt gossip.

When the protectee is a speaker, the BG should position

himself so that he is facing the audience and off to the side so that he can watch the wings of the stage as well as the audience. A bullet-resistant podium should be used to offer maximum protection.

When attending plays, operas, or sporting events, box seats offer a certain degree of privacy and limit access. Ballistic panels can be placed in a theater box in advance to offer greater protection against bullets or blast. If the box is curtained, the heavy curtain will offer some protection against thrown objects other than incendiaries. If only one BG is available, he should sit inside the box at the rear. If two BGs are on duty, one can be outside the door.

If a box is not available and regular seats are used, the BG should be seated directly behind the protectee. Additional BGs should sit at the two ends of the protectee's row. If enough BGs are available, one should sit in the back row so that he can observe anyone making a hostile move towards the protectee.

When escorting the protectee to any of these functions vehicular security and escort drills to and from the building should be followed as discussed under vehicular security.

7. MINIMIZING THE THREAT

A GOOD PORTION OF THE BG'S JOB involves anticipating possible risks and countering them in advance or making sure they are countered through others such as local law enforcement agencies. This may necessitate the BG training servants, secretaries, and family members of the protectee in possible security risks so that they can avoid them. If the protectee is employed by a large corporation or owns his own corporation which has a security director, the BG will need to work with him to anticipate possible problems at the place of business.

As is discussed in the chapter on vehicular security, patterns which place the protectee at the same location at the same time should be avoided whenever possible, since patterns allow kidnappers or assassins the opportunity to choose their own time and place for an attack. Even such routines as church attendance should be varied, attending different services and even occasionally different churches.

A good driver should also anticipate possible attacks. He should arrive early to pick up his employer if he doesn't wait for him or doesn't live in and should use the few minutes while waiting to check the area out for anything suspicious. The driver should be especially alert for cars following the vehicle he is driving. If the protectee drives himself, he should avoid parking at the office in parking spaces marked with his name or title. (Note: Some high-risk targets still prefer the privacy of driving their own vehicles while the BG or BGs follow in another car. Normally, this is not sound procedure, however, since it is obviously much easier to separate the protectee from his protector in this case.) The well-trained VIP chauffeur will normally avoid such executive parking spaces unless their closeness to an entrance or exit outweighs the fact they compromise the identity of the vehicle's occupant. I have often advised that there be certain parking spaces marked for a seemingly middle-level employee, such as the assistant personnel director, which are actually VIP parking places. It may also be a good idea for the VIP chauffeur to occasionally pull over to the side of the road and sit for a minute just to check if the vehicle is being followed.

Family, business associates, and servants should be thoroughly trained not to give information to strangers or the press which could compromise security. I once insisted that a servant be fired because she had sold information which could have compromised a high-threat protectee's security to a scandal sheet reporter. Even if the information had been innocuous, I would still have had the servant fired since she was obviously unreliable. Personal details such as what country club the protectee belongs to or that he's a season ticket holder to the opera should be kept secret since such information can place him at a certain place at a certain time. Staff members and family should be especially careful about revealing the protectee's travel plans and itinerary. Even the practice of publishing the protectee's photograph in the business or society pages should be discouraged since this aids an attacker in identifying his target. If a photograph is an absolute requirement for a corporation press release using one that is outdated and doesn't look too much like the protectee is desirable.

The BG should make sure that all household and office employees who work closely with the protectee or have access to information about him have had a security check. He should have some sort of signal system to let the BG or secretary know he is under duress. A simple telephone code can also be agreed upon. One of the simplest can be based on the method in which he announces who he is. First name alone can mean one thing, while title and last name can mean another, and first and last name can mean another still. Just last name alone could have a fourth meaning. Many executive briefcases, in fact, are equipped with a "beeper" which allows the owner to be traced if he's kidnapped. The protectee should also learn to be watchful of strangers and not to arrange meetings with strangers at isolated locations. On this point, it should be noted that more than one kidnapping or assassination took place when the protectee slipped away to visit a mistress. Meetings kept secret from the BG are an invitation to an attacker. Both VIP and BG should also dress as much as possible to blend into the milieu in foreign countries. There is no need to incite an attack by obviously appearing as rich foreigners, although dress should not become a masquerade.

The BG should always anticipate the possibility of an ambush and alert a secretary or member of the family of the estimated time the protectee is to arrive somewhere. If the BG doesn't check in on time, this person can then be prepared to call for assistance. Since most VIP cars are equipped with either a two-way radio or a radio telephone, such calls for assistance can normally be made from the vehicle, but there is the possibility of the vehicle's battery being knocked out. VIP cars with obvious communications antennas are a dead giveaway to terrorists since such antennas usually indicate a VIP.

Employees can be briefed to take note of any suspicious persons lurking around an estate or office. License numbers, descriptions, or, when surveillance cameras are around, video tapes should be noted.

The BG normally does not have time to check his employer's mail every day, but both secretaries and household staff can be briefed on detecting letter or package bombs. Compact, reasonably inexpensive X-ray or other types of mechanical detection devices are available to check mail. If at all possible, one should be installed in the home and another one in the office. Currently, highly sophisticated computerized "bomb sniffers" are available. Although there are portable detection devices which can be easily transported, the BG and also staff members need to be cognizant of how to check for letter or package bombs even without the aid of a mechanical detector.

Tipoffs which should draw the attention of security people are:

- no return address or a smudged or blurred return address
- an address composed of letters clipped from a magazine or newspaper
- an oddly wrapped or sealed package
- an envelope seeming heavier than normal for the thickness of paper it probably contains
- greasy marks or stains on the envelope possibly caused by the explosive sweating (especially in hot climates)
- an odd smell, especially of bitter almonds
- the letter or parcel feeling lopsided with the weight unevenly distributed
- the envelope and contents not having the normal crinkly feel, or feeling as if the envelope is stuck to the contents
- the outline of the trigger mechanism—often a small coin-shaped camera battery—that can be felt inside the envelope, usually at the logical point of opening
- care must be taken not to apply undue pressure to the package in case a pressure sensitive detonator is used.

Sonic bomb detectors can also be used since they pick up the sound of a clockwork detonator.

Being familiar with the techniques taught at the various training centers for "national liberation fronts" may be useful for the BG since he may have to counter their techniques. That's one of the real advantages of Special Forces, SAS, or other counter-terrorist training; former members of these units learn the curriculums of the Lenin Institute, Pankow, Karlovy Vary, Ras Hilal, and Torca.

The good BG should also know the terrorist groups which operate in any countries where he's likely to be working. By knowing both their philosophies and methodology, the BG can decide first, if the protectee is a likely target, and second, what form the attack is likely to take. Between 1972 and 1978, for example, 16 FIAT executives were kidnapped, murdered, or wounded. Obviously, the BG guarding a FIAT exec would want to take special precautions and thoroughly know Red Brigade techniques. Since 1974, over four thousand executives have been kidnapped and held for ransom. Just in the small country of Colombia, kidnappings of executives at one point reached three a day. Obviously, the smart BG would try to keep his client clear of Colombia, but if a visit were absolutely necessary extreme caution would be called for.

Keeping up with terrorist groups is no mean feat. Just to name a few which have been active during the last ten years, one would need information on:

MIR—Chile
ELN—Bolivia
ERP—Argentina
FALN—Puerto Rico
Tupamaros—Uruguay
M19—Colombia
FLQ—Quebec
Moro National Liberation Front—Philippines
Japanese Red Army—originally Japan, but now Middle
                               East with the Palestinians

PFLP—Western Europe and Middle East
Baader Meinhof Gang—W. Germany
IRA (Provisional Wing)—UK
ETA (Basque Movement)—Spain, occasionally France
Red Brigade—Italy
SLA—USA
Montoneros—Argentina
ARC—France
TPLA—Turkey
Armenian Secret Army—Turkish targets worldwide

Some of these groups have virtually ceased to exist, and new groups come into existence each year. Many of these groups, especially in Latin America, use VIP kidnappings as their principal source of income. The ERP in Argentina, for example, earned $14.2 million for a kidnapped Exxon executive. That much money will buy a lot of security. Ransom insurance is fine, but it encourages kidnapping. Tough professional BGs discourage kidnappings. Less than one percent of high-risk kidnapping targets have adequate security, and many have no security at all. As a result, a well-protected individual will usually be left alone since there are plenty of "soft" targets out there.

The BG must also be aware that there are many government-sponsored terrorist organizations which generate many jobs for BGs. Libyan hit squads do exist, and former members of the Libyan royal family (among others) hire BGs specifically to counter this threat. Iranian hit squads have also created a boom market for BGs among former members of the hierarchy under the Shah. In some parts of the world and when working for some employers, the Israeli Mossad is classed as a terrorist organization. The BG needs to be familiar with these government assassins and their methods as well as the free-lance terrorists.

The BG's knowledge of countries shouldn't stop with

possible terrorist groups. One needs to know how much co-operation one can expect from the local police and whether or not they are corrupt. In some countries, the police sympathize with one political faction and may even give terrorists from that faction active assistance. Most good international BGs have cultivated many police contacts, which can prove useful. Assuming one is working in a country with supportive law enforcement officials, then photographs of likely attackers should be obtained for study. The good BG should also check into the qualifications of any local police officers assigned to protective duties since normal police training does not qualify one for protective assignments.

If the protectee is a likely assassination target, the BG should do everything possible to convince him to wear light-weight body armor. A firm in Israel makes excellent sports clothing which contains Kevlar 29 layers. Sportcoats or top-coats are also available from other sources or a police style t-shirt ballistic vest can be used. If the employer does not want to wear the vest at all times, he should wear one when in crowds or other high-threat environments. The BG, too, should wear a vest both for his own protection and for his employer's since he will be shielding the protectee with his own body. Vests give a certain amount of protection from weapons other than guns, too. My vest once turned a knife, and vests have stopped grenade fragments. Some BGs also carry an overcoat which has been designed of ballistic nylon and coated with a fire retardant substance to act as a "bomb blanket." Such coats weigh between fifteen and twenty-five pounds and can be thrown over a grenade or other explosive device hurled at the protectee to contain much of the blast. Another technique used by some BGs is carrying briefcases lined with bullet-resistant material. Three or four BGs who have practiced using their briefcases can form a ballistic "wall" around the vital areas of the protectee while moving between a vehicle and building.

Another important element of threat anticipation is to always have an escape route planned. The good BG notes alternate exits from buildings, alternate routes when driving, etc. Although it's not possible 100 percent of the time, the BG should strive to have an escape plan in mind wherever his charge is. As simple as it sounds, a good BG carries a small flashlight for use in maneuvering out of buildings which have had the power cut, either intentionally or unintentionally. The smart BG also always has the right change available for a pay phone, should an emergency call be necessary.

All BGs should have first-aid training, but if the protectee has a special medical problem (i.e. epilepsy, heart trouble, etc.) which would require immediate action, the BG should know what immediate action to take. For example, I once guarded a client who had only a few minutes in which to receive an antivenom shot if stung by a bee.

Another piece of anticipatory security is to have another professional, whose abilities one trusts, look over the security set-up and offer opinions on how he would crack it. It's surprising how often an "impenetrable" area security system has a flaw that is so obvious it is overlooked. The BG should also note flaws in security precautions of other VIPs or of places passed through—such as airports. These lapses on the part of other security personnel can expose the protectee to danger if he is expected to rely upon them. King Hussein of Jordan, for example, has the perfect solution in countries where the hosts do not want him or his BGs armed and expect him to rely upon them entirely. The King politely agrees and wears his H&K P7 in an ankle holster. Hussein hasn't survived so many assassination attempts by placing too much faith in security forces other than his own.

Speaking of Hussein, though, raises another point: should the protectee be armed himself? Unlike some "executive

protection specialists" (i.e. former members of one of the
bureaucratic federal or local law enforcement agencies, with
former members of the NYPD or New Scotland Yard being
the worst) who abhor the thought of a "civilian" going around
armed, I see nothing wrong with the protectee being armed
in case of a "worst case scenario." I have worked for many
individuals who are constantly armed, and in some parts of
the world, because of the "machismo" of firearms, it is almost
certain any VIP will be armed. If working for an employer
who either carries or keeps a weapon in his home or office,
I do, however, attempt to assure myself that the protectee
is competent with the weapon. I want to evaluate the likelihood of my employer panicking and shooting someone by
mistake—such as his BG. If the employer insists on his own
weapon and is completely incompetent with it, I train him
in its use. If the employer will not accept such training, he
may well be shopping for a new BG. I have found, however,
that most VIPs purchasing a firearm are thankful for training from a competent instructor and take full advantage of
the opportunity to use the weapon well.

Although protection against electronic eavesdropping
devices is discussed only in passing in this book, having both
the protectee's residence and office frequently swept for bugs
is a good idea since useful information to a terrorist or kidnapper can be gained from such devices. (Business secrets,
etc. could also be gained but protecting such information is
not normally the BG's job.)

Although firearms training is discussed elsewhere in this
book, certain elements of weapons use are also preventive.
The BG, for example, must get used to performing two functions at once—shielding his charge with his body or getting
him under cover and preparing to engage the attacker with
fire. Unless one practices this dual reaction assiduously, it
is very easy to jump for cover under pressure leaving the

protectee in the open or to go into a "gunfighter's crouch" leaving the employer's head and torso exposed. Practicing with either a mannequin or an associate helps anticipate this situation and inculcates shielding into the proper reaction.

To summarize in simple terms, the good BG anticipates possible avenues of attack and areas of vulnerability and then either acts to eliminate or reduce the times and places where and when the protectee will be vulnerable. The BG must attempt to gain as much information about potential attackers as possible (including studying psychological and behavioral profiles of typical assassins so that their behavior might be spotted), while doing everything he can to limit the information potential attackers can gain about his employer. Though always striving for strong preventive security, the BG realizes that no system is foolproof and plans in advance alternate escape routes and reactions to certain types of attack. Of course, no plan should become so setpiece that flexibility in the face of unsuspected danger is lost.

Other Paladin Press books by Leroy Thompson:

Commando Dagger: The Complete Illustrated
  History of the Fairbairn-Sykes Fighting Knife

De Oppresso Liber: The Illustrated History
  of the U. S. Army Special Forces

The Rescuers: The World's Top Anti-Terrorist
  Units

Survival/Fighting Knives